Why Learn Game Theory?

Game theory is a beautiful subject and this book will teach you how to understand the theory and practically implement solutions. This book has two primary objectives.

(1) To help you recognize strategic situations.

(2) To show you how to make better decisions and *change the game*, a powerful concept that can transform no-win situations into mutually beneficial outcomes.

As these goals indicate, game theory is about more than board games and gambling. Specifically, game theory is a branch of economics that considers how players of a mathematically formalized game can optimize their decisions. In these games, what each person does has an effect on other people in the group. Game theory studies how to make the best choice in situations of interdependent decision-making.

Game theory offers practical insights that have been applied to various fields, including political science, business, evolutionary biology, computer science, and philosophy. The Nobel Prize in Economics was awarded for work in game theory in the years 1994 (John C. Harsanyi, John F. Nash Jr. and Reinhard Selten), 2005 (Robert J. Aumann and Thomas C. Schelling), 2007 (Leonid Hurwicz, Eric S. Maskin and Roger B. Myerson), and 2012 (Alvin E. Roth and Lloyd S. Shapley).

Before proceeding, it is worth providing a functional definition. In this book, a *game* will mean a situation characterized by three components: (1) a set of people involved called *players*, (2), a set of allowable moves that each player can make, known as *strategies*, and (3) a description of how each player feels about the possible outcomes mathematically described by a *payoff* or *utility function*.

It all seems so simple, and yet that definition belies the complexity of game theory. While it may only take a few seconds to define what a game is, it takes a lifetime to appreciate and master game theory. This book will get you started.

Section I: Introducing Strategic Games

This section opens with several examples of game theory and defines basic concepts, such as a dominant strategy and a Nash equilibrium. The goal is to get familiar with how games are described and solved, and how game theory is relevant for everyday situations.

Unlike a textbook approach where one learns definitions and theories first, this book is based on understanding strategy with real-life situations and stories. We will jump right in with a puzzle about why gas stations tend to cluster in location.

Why Are Gas Stations Often Located Next To Each Other?

There are hundreds of gas stations around San Francisco in the California Bay Area. One might think that gas stations would spread out to serve local neighborhoods. But this idea is contradicted by a common observation. Whenever you visit a gas station, there is almost always another in the vicinity, often just across the street. In general, gas stations are highly clustered.

The phenomenon is partly due to population clustering. Gas stations will be more common where demand is high, like in a city, rather than in sparsely populated areas like cornfields. But why do stations locate right across the street from each other? Why don't they spread out?

There are many factors at play. Locating a gas station is an optimization problem involving demand, real estate prices, estimates of population growth, and supply considerations such as the ease of refueling. As the problem is complex, any simplified explanation will have its shortcomings.

Nevertheless, there is a simple game about location competition that provides valuable insight. While the game involves only a few rules, it illustrates how businesses might compete on location and end up clustering together. The game also has an application to political science in the strategy for campaigning in elections. The following game is based on a model described in the 1929 paper "Stability in Competition" by the mathematician Harold Hotelling.

Hotelling's Game

There are two players in this game. In this exposition, imagine each player is a hot dog stand on a beach that competes for customers. The beach is a straight shoreline, in which customers are uniformly spread out. The beach is represented by a number line ranging from -1 at one endpoint to 1 at the other.

The hot dog stands compete purely on location and sell identical products. Each stand picks a location, which is represented by a number between -1 and 1.

Conditional on where the stands locate, customers will simply choose the stand closer to them. If the stands are in the same spot, customers will split up and both stands end up with an equal number of customers. For instance, if a customer is at point 0.5, and the stands are located at -1 and 1, the customer will be closer and choose the stand located at point 1.

The following figure is a graphical representation of the game, with the labels S_1 and S_2 for the locations of hot dog stands 1 and 2, respectively. Note the endpoints of the shore and the placeholders for each stand's location.

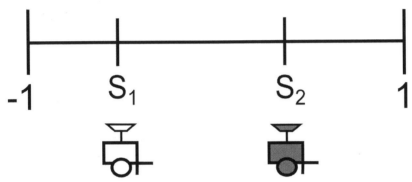

If the two hot dog stands compete for the most customers, where will each hot dog stand end up? (For reference, the solution to the game is referred to as a *Nash equilibrium*, which will be explained in subsequent chapters).

Finding The Solution (Intuitive)

One way to approach the game is to ignore the competition. Assume you are the only hot dog stand on the beach. Where might you want to locate?

The answer is easy: any place you want. You are a monopolist so customers will have to walk to you regardless. If you choose to locate all the way at one endpoint -1, customers even from the other side of the beach at endpoint 1 will have to walk all the way. For you, it is nice to be a monopoly.

But you are a paranoid monopoly, and common sense would push you closer to the center, labeled point 0. The problem is that if you locate all the way on the far left, or all the way on the far right, a competitor might choose a more central location and cut you off. If you favor the left side, for instance, an entrant could locate slightly to your right, closer to the center, and capture the majority of the market.

See the following figure where the market share of the monopoly (solid line segment) is overtaken by a new entrant (dashed line segment).

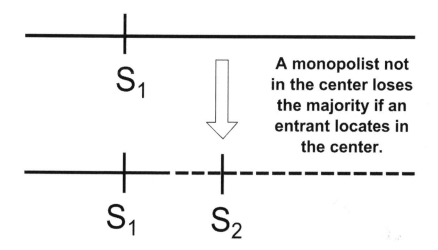

S_1

A monopolist not in the center loses the majority if an entrant locates in the center.

S_1 S_2

Such a problem does not happen if you locate in the center. A new entrant to either your left or right side would gain less than half the market.

The logic shows why the center point is favorable. Furthermore, note that if either hot dog stand chooses the center point, the other will want to copy, since it is better to split the market than end up on one side that yields less than half the market.

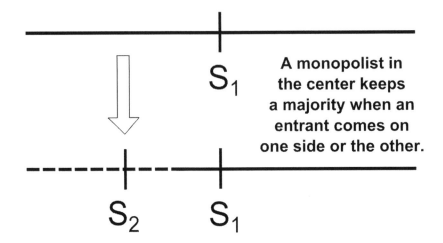

S_1

A monopolist in
the center keeps
a majority when an
entrant comes on
one side or the other.

S_2 S_1

The above logic is correct but not mathematically precise. To develop a fuller appreciation for game theory, it is necessary to wade through a mathematical argument. This is not necessary for reading the book and understanding game theory, but it is presented here as a taste of a mathematical proof. As such, I highly encourage you to at least skim through this section. If you do choose to skip it, continue reading at the section labeled "The Social Optimum."

Finding The Solution (Mathematical)

Each hot dog stand is simultaneously picking a location, a number between -1 and 1.

Each stand needs to take into account where the other might locate. That's the key factor in game theory—decisions are interdependent.

I will break the problem down into two steps. This is a process you can use to solve other games.

Step 1: Think About Payoffs

Imagine the two stands locate at points 0.2 and 0.4. How much of the beach would each stand capture?

You can see it in the following figure. It indicates the segments of the beach where the customers are closer to the first stand (solid line segment) or to the second stand (dashed line segment).

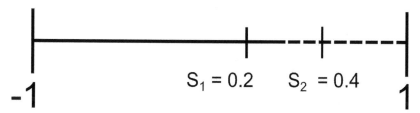

$S_1 = 0.2$ $S_2 = 0.4$

-1   1

Here is how I came up with that picture. The first stand clearly gets any customer located at a point less than 0.2 (the left), and the second hot dog stand gets any customer standing at a point higher than 0.4 (the right). Halfway between the two stands, at the point 0.3, is where customers are equally happy. Therefore, anyone standing at a numerical value larger than the halfway point goes to the stand at 0.4, and anyone standing at a numerical value less than the halfway point goes to the stand at 0.2.

The lengths of the solid and dashed lines represent the market shares of each hot dog stand. In this example, the first stand gets 65% of the line compared to 35% for the second.

This arrangement of the stands, however, is not a solution to the game, as it is possible for one of the stands to find a better position. For example, if the second stand inches closer to the middle, say, at the point 0.2, then both stands would be equally desirable options for the customers, and they would split the market 50% to each. But that again is not a solution to the game, as the first stand could then retaliate by moving even closer to the center point to get more customers.

There is a mathematical way to describe how each stand would react to the other's choice.

Step 2: Determine The Best Responses

A best response is a location that one stand would choose optimally in response to a given position of the other stand's location. More generally, a best response is a strategy that one player would choose in response to the given strategy profile of another player, or a group of players.

To simplify matters, instead of dealing with market share percentages, consider the game as one that a hot dog stand can either win or lose. Imagine a hot dog stand "wins" the game by having a majority of the market.

Suppose the first stand chooses a location k. What is a best response for second stand? What are the locations that will capture over half of the market?

There is not a single answer. As explained earlier, anything closer to the center will capture a majority of the market. These are points that are less than distance k from the center, corresponding to numbers between the values $-k$ and k.

Here is a diagram of the best response for a given location.

If $S_1 = k$ then the best response is S_2 anywhere in the dashed region

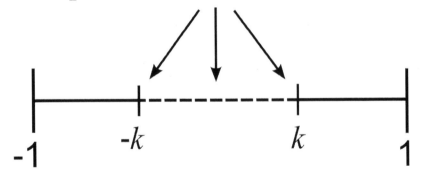

If one player chooses $k = 0$, the center point, then the unique best response is to pick the center point as well.

This is the solution of the game: when both pick the center, both are playing best responses to each other. The two hot dog stands will split the market evenly.

The Social Optimum

Game theory suggests an outcome for what players will do. But that is unfortunately not always the best outcome for society. The equilibrium of the hot dog game is an annoying situation for many customers. The hot dog stands are located in the center of the beach instead of spreading out and being closer to beachgoers.

In fact, if the stands could be spaced out across the entire beach (at points -0.50 and 0.50) then everyone would be happier. Since the stands are spread out, each would still get 50% of the market. The advantage to this location is that the stands are located closer to more customers: no customer would have to travel more than a distance of 0.50 to reach a hot dog stand. In the solution where both stands are at 0, the customers at the endpoints have to walk a distance of 1.

A Social Optimum

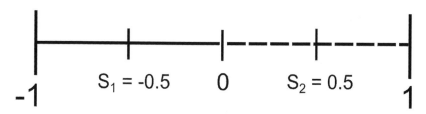

As desirable as this outcome is, it is not sustainable. The reason is that each stand has an incentive to deviate. Either one could choose to locate closer to the center and gain more than half the customers. The other stand would retaliate by moving closer to the center as well, and the game would go on until both end up in the center.

Gas Stations And Other Examples

The model explains the strategy of why competitors locate so close to each other and compete on real estate. Think about burger chains, supermarkets, and coffee shops. You will almost always see them clustered even though it would be nicer for customers if they spread out.

The model can also be applied to political candidates. Imagine two candidates picking a platform on a political spectrum from -1 (very liberal) to 1 (very conservative). If voters pick the candidate closest to their own political views, and voters are spread out across the political spectrum, then both candidates have an incentive to converge to the middle, moderate position. It is no surprise that politicians seek the "average vote." The game also explains why it is so hard to tell the difference between candidates while they are campaigning for an election.

A final application of this game is local TV news. Note that local news channels compete for attention, and each chooses a set of stories during a given show. It would be nice if different news stations talked about different topics, but that does not happen. We end up with the same story being reported on virtually all news outlets instead of having hundreds of different important stories being reported. How many times have you watched a local news report about one story, and then switched to another channel to see exactly the same story reported? Surprisingly they all are covering the same news in the same order, as news stations converge in reporting the most interesting stories. As a concluding note, that is one reason the web has been liberating. Entry is cheap, so blogs and websites can serve smaller interests, allowing for niche topics to get increased coverage.

Could Price Match Guarantees Help Businesses Instead Of You?

When a store advertises it will match the price of any competitor, it sounds like the store is offering a good deal. Not only are they confident their prices are the lowest, but if you find a lower price anywhere else, they will even match it. The apparent winner of a price matching policy is the consumer.

In fact, that is how price matching is often reported in the news. For example, an article in *The Wall Street Journal* on November 2013 predicted a "looming price war" between electronics retailers who pledged to match prices of competitors during the holiday shopping season.

But does price matching always mean more competition and lower prices? One would have to do a detailed study of prices to understand the full effects of price matching. But even without that, a game theory model can suggest how price matching might affect prices. One game paradoxically suggests price matching can do the opposite: it can help prices stay high!

Monopoly (One Business)

Consider a hypothetical example where Lears is a monopolist and makes refrigerators at a cost of $200. Lacking competition, Lears can raise the selling price of the refrigerator until it maximizes revenue. Say this price is $300. Lears is happy, but society would be better off with a lower price.

Duopoly (Two Businesses)

Lucky for the consumer, Sowe's has decided to enter the market and it is able to make an identical refrigerator for the same cost of $200.

What price should Sowe's set? If it sets a price of $300, then customers will be indifferent to both companies, so Sowe's will acquire half of the market and split the profits with Lears. But if Sowe's sets a lower price of $299, all consumers will prefer the lower price and switch to that store. Sowe's will effectively capture the entire market at a price just lower than the monopoly price.

But Lears will not be happy to lose all of its customers. It would respond by an even lower price of $298 so that it can recapture the market. Since the firms cannot trust each other and simply agree on a price because of anti-trust laws, they are forced to compete. Ultimately, both firms keep bidding the down the price until the price drops all the way to $200. At this point, both businesses would lose money by lowering the price so they will not do that. And neither can raise the price, as the other company would then be cheaper.

The game presented above is known as the *Bertrand Duopoly*. It is characterized by two firms competing solely on price to customers that have no loyalty and simply pick the firm with the lowest price.

It is often thought that a market with just a few firms will have high prices, as the firms will collude to keep profits high. The stunning result of the Bertrand Duopoly model is that a market with only two firms can end up competing to the lowest price due to a bidding war.

How you feel about that largely depends on your perspective. Someone that comparison shops is happy with the result since it means lower prices. Someone that runs a business is scared that prices drop down, and that is why businesses refer to the "ruinous effects of a price war."

Ideally businesses would hope to keep prices high for everyone so they could share larger profits. And it turns out that price matching is a policy that could allow them to do precisely that.

How Price Matching Affects The Game

One thing to note is the Bertrand Duopoly model does not mean heavily concentrated markets are price competitive. Businesses do not simply compete on price for customers; they take actions to maintain profits by locking in customers and trying to increase loyalty. Theoretically, a price match guarantee could also help businesses keep prices high.

To see why, suppose Sowe's and Lears advertise price matching policies, and even offer an extra 10% of the price difference. That sure seems pro-consumer, but how are the firms' incentives changed?

Recall that at first Lears and Sowe's both start with a price of $300. They split the market and have healthy profits. In the standard Bertrand Duopoly, each competes by lowering the price to gain customers. But with price matching guarantees at both stores, will a bidding war begin?

What happens if Sowe's decides to lower its price to $299? When Sowe's lowers its prices, customers would not actually go to Sowe's. They would choose to shop at Lears and get an additional discount from the price matching policy. In essence, when Sowe's lowers its price, it cannot gain customers as it did in the standard Bertrand Duopoly.

In effect, price matching has ruined the incentive to create a bidding war, and the bidding war will never start! Both firms have tacitly cooperated to keep prices high.

Credible Threats

There are also other reasons a store might institute a price matching policy. For one, it is a good public relations technique. Businesses want to say, "Don't go to my competition. I have the lowest price." But there is no reason to trust a business whose main motivation is to profit.

So a business could try to make the claim more credible with a price matching policy. The policy has the effect of a business saying, "Look, I have the lowest price. I'm so sure of it, just look at my price matching policy. Heck, I'll even give you a 10% discount." Now that sure sounds nice.

The positive image of price matching guarantees is perhaps one reason why most stores have them. And while we feel like all the stores are helping us, it is possible they are using price matching as a subtle method to increase profits.

Source

Fitzgerald, Drew, and Paul Ziobro. "Price War Looms for Electronics." *The Wall Street Journal*. 20 Nov 2013. Web. http://online.wsj.com/news/articles/SB10001424052702303755045792083820 32930724.

Dominated Strategies

We will now change gears. The first examples in this book have been about business applications. But game theory is a tool for making smart decisions any time, as the following story illustrates.

One night I was trying to catch a cab in San Francisco. I decided it best to go near a popular intersection but stay away from the crowd. I was lucky and soon a cab approached. Just as I was getting in, a woman complained she was outside first and I was "stealing" her cab. I politely replied that I had not seen her, but since another cab was coming after mine, she should hail that cab. She scowled before taking my advice.

I recounted the incident from the cab. I was particularly puzzled as to why she was yelling at me. If she was primarily concerned with getting a cab, it seemed yelling was about the worst thing she could do.

Why is that? It's because she needed to think about the game from *my perspective*. You see, since I was closer to the approaching cab, I had full control to take the cab. Given that, she had a range of choices to increase her chances of getting a cab. She could have asked me politely to give up the cab, moved to another location, or even called a cab on her phone. All of these choices would have improved her chances of getting a cab. But by yelling instead, she rubbed me the wrong way and lowered her chances.

In game theory, when a player's action (like her yelling) leads to a worse outcome than another action (her hailing the other cab going by), for every possible way other players decide to act (in each situation, the chance I would give her the cab), the action is said to be **dominated.**

There is an obvious lesson from game theory: never choose a dominated action. If you learn one thing from this book, let this be the lesson: **please, never, never play dominated strategies.**

Dominated strategies are not just bad decisions; they are the worst possible decisions. Buying lottery tickets is a losing bet and generally not smart, but even then you have a chance to win. So you can think of playing a dominated strategy as worse than buying a lottery ticket. You are always better off avoiding dominated strategies.

Winning A "Beauty Contest"

The idea of not picking dominated strategies sounds simple, but the theoretical prediction is not always the same as the practical outcome. I will illustrate this with an example when I was a student at Stanford. In a memorable lecture, my game theory professor staked $250 to teach a lesson about crowd behavior.

The lecture began innocently enough. We were going to play a simple game with the following rules.

1. Everyone would secretly submit a whole number from 0 to 20.

2. All entries would be collected and averaged together.

3. The winning number would be chosen as *two-thirds of the average*, rounded to the closest number. For instance, if the average of all entries was 3, then the winning number would be chosen as 2. Or if the average was 4, the winning number would be 3 (rounded from 2.66...).

4. Entries closest to the winning number would get a prize of meeting with the professor over a $5 smoothie. (The textbook version of the game has multiple winners *split* the prize. My professor was being generous).

Before you read on, I would like you to seriously consider what number you might pick. Imagine you are sitting in a lecture hall and actually playing this game. You seek the glory of outsmarting 49 other students, and you really want to meet with the professor since you find game theory fascinating. You have 10 seconds to decide before ballots are collected. Which number would you pick?

Some Guiding Logic

The game is called a "p-beauty contest." The "p" refers to the proportion the average is multiplied by—in this case, p is two-thirds. It turns out the game has a similar outcome for any value of p less than 1. Why is it called a beauty contest? The name is because the game is the numbers-analog to a beauty contest developed by John Maynard Keynes.

Imagine a newspaper runs a contest to determine the prettiest face in town. Readers can vote for the prettiest face, and the face with the most votes will be the winner. Readers voting for the prettiest face will be entered in a raffle for a big prize.

How does the game play out? Keynes wanted to point out the group dynamics. The naive strategy would be to pick the face *you* found to be the most attractive. A better strategy would be to pick the face that you thought *other* people would find attractive.

The number "beauty contest" has the same kind of logic. You do not pick a number you like. You should pick a number based on what others will pick, so that your number is closest to two-thirds of the average. The twist of both games is that your guess affects the average outcome. And each person is trying to outsmart everyone else.

Given the subtlety of the game, my professor was banking on paying out to only a few winners. Although it was mathematically possible for each of us to win, he was taking that risk. In fact, he knew that if we were all rational, we would all win. He would have to pay out a $5 smoothie to 50 students—that is, he made a $250 gamble playing this game.

Why was he so confident? Let us explore the solution to the game and see why it is hard to be logically rational.

Numbers You Should Not Pick

Even though it is not possible to know what other people are guessing, this game has a solution. If everyone acts completely logically, there are only two possible winning numbers. It takes some crafty thinking, but the result is based on two principles I think you will accept.

Principle 1: Do Not Play Stupid Strategies (Eliminate Dominated Strategies)

The first principle is that players should avoid writing down numbers that could never win. That sounds logical enough, but it is not always the case. We can all agree that writing a number that could never win is a very bad strategy. You are picking an option that is inferior to something else, which if you recall, is called a dominated strategy.

Are there any dominated strategies in the beauty contest?

To answer that question, we need to figure out which numbers would never win. A natural question is: what is the highest winning number? You would never want to pick a number *larger* than that, unless you wanted to lose.

You know that the highest number anyone can pick is the number 20. If every single person picked 20, then the average would be 20. The winning number would be two-thirds of 20, which is 13 when rounded.

Should you ever find yourself submitting 20?

The answer is no—there is always a better choice, like the number 19. The only time 20 wins is precisely when everyone else picks it and everyone shares the prize. In that case, you would be better off writing 19 to win the prize unshared. Plus, by writing 19, you can possibly win in other cases, like when everyone else picks 19. You are always better off writing 19 than 20. The guess of 20 is a dominated strategy.

You should never choose 20. And your rational opponents should be thinking the same way. So here is the big result: you can reason that *no player would ever choose 20.*

Principle 2: Trim The Game And Iterate

By principle 1, no player would ever choose 20. Therefore, you can essentially remove 20 as a choice. The game trims to a smaller beauty contest in which everyone is picking a number between 0 and 19. The smaller game has survived one round of principle 1.

Now, repeat! Ask yourself: in the reduced game, are there any dominated strategies?

Now 19 takes the role of 20 from the last analysis. Since 19 is the highest possible average, it will never be a good idea to guess it. Applying principle 1, you can reason that 18 is always a better choice than 19. Thus, 19 is dominated and should be eliminated as a choice for every player.

The game is now trimmed to picking numbers from 0 to 18. This is the result of two iterations of principle 1.

There is no reason to stop now. You can iterate principle 1 to successively eliminate the choices of 18, 17, 16, and so on. The process ends after eliminating all numbers except 0 and 1.

This thought process is aptly named *iterated elimination of dominated strategies (IEDS)*. The idea is to eliminate bad moves, trim the game, and iterate the process. The surviving moves are known as *rationalizable* strategies because they can possibly win. Here is a schematic for IEDS.

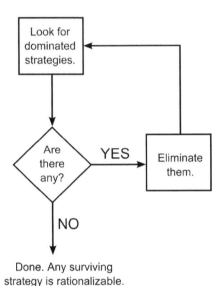

Done. Any surviving
strategy is rationalizable.

The Equilibria

The only strategies that survive IEDS are the numbers 0 and 1. Is either a better choice? This is unfortunately where IEDS cannot give insight.

It is possible to have 0 as a winning number. If all 50 students picked 0, then the winning number would be 0.

Similarly, it is possible to have 1 as a winning number. If all 50 students picked 1, then the winning number would be 2/3, which rounds to 1.

What actually happens depends on what people think everyone else will be guessing. Both equilibria—all 0 and all 1—are achievable.

Back To The Classroom

None of us in the class had this deep understanding of IEDS. We were just learning game theory—it was actually our third lecture. My professor was pretty sure our guesses would be all over the place.

But Stanford kids can be crafty. One student used some sharp thinking and realized that coordination would help; he asked if we could talk to each other. The professor, still feeling we were novices, confidently replied with a smile, "Sure. Go ahead." We only had 10 seconds to write down our answers anyway.

Before the professor could change his mind, the student quickly shouted to all of us, "If we all write down 0, we all win."

It was remarkable. He figured out the equilibrium and told us what to do! He couldn't be tricking us because the math was clear: if we all picked 0, we would all have winning numbers.

How Smart Are Stanford Kids?

The professor was relieved after he tallied the votes. He told us that admirably most of us wrote down the number 0 (I was among those who did). But there were larger answers too, ranging from 1 to 10.

Someone actually wrote down 10! And this was after being told the answer.

After all was said and done, the winning number turned out to be 2, and the prize was awarded to three students. Thanks to our lack of coordination, my professor only paid out a prize of $15.

It was even better. My professor questioned the students who wrote down larger numbers. They all squirmed and explained reasons like "it was my lucky number" or "I don't know. I wasn't really thinking."

The Practical Lesson

What is going on? This is a group of smart students that was told the answer to the game.

The example illustrates a flaw of IEDS. It can get you reasonable answers if you think players are reasoning out further and further in nested logic. We often do not have an infinite capacity to reason logically, only a bounded ability to reason rationality.

The practical answer to what you should write depends on the book answer plus your subjective *beliefs* about what other people do. It is the combination of book smarts plus social smarts that matters.

The people who wrote down the winning numbers told the class they suspected some people would deviate for irrational reasons. And they were rewarded for not confusing theory with practice.

Dominant Strategies

A *dominated* strategy is one that you should never play. The flip side is a *dominant* strategy, a strategy that always makes sense and should be played. A dominant strategy is one that gives you the best outcome, regardless of what your other choices are and what other people are doing.

A simple example is when you are choosing the best checkout line in a store. Say there are two lines A and B with equally competent cashiers. You see that line A has a wait of one person while line B has no wait. What should you do? It is clear that you should go to line B where there is no wait: this is a dominant strategy.

A more nuanced example is picking the best lane while driving. Imagine the right lane has one car in front of you while the left lane has no cars, and there are no other cars around. All you want to do is drive straight for several miles. What do you do? Picking the left lane is generally a better option: the person in the right lane might drive slowly, or they might slow down to turn at an intersection. In this example, picking the left lane is a dominant strategy.

Some examples of dominant strategies are obvious. But others are harder to see. A few years ago, I was running errands and remembered I needed to visit the bank. But the time was 5:02pm, so I was not sure if the bank had closed already.

I was debating whether to take a few minutes to drive by my bank, or to take care of other errands, one which would take 20 minutes and the other 40 minutes. I wanted to get everything done, and I really wanted to start off succeeding in my first task. Which one should I do first?

a. Check the bank.
b. Do the 20 minute errand.
c. Do the 40 minute errand.

The answer is not difficult, and in fact you can probably figure it out without knowledge of game theory. But I find the situation is instructive for the idea of a dominant strategy.

Dominant Strategies

I was with my dad who instantly came up with the proper decision (I jokingly said it's because I've taught him some game theory).

The proper decision is to do the 20 minute errand first. Why? Consider the likely times the bank would close.

Case 1: The bank already closed at 5:00. The choice of checking the bank first is bad since I wanted to succeed in my first task.

Case 2: The bank closes at 5:30. Within 30 minutes I could check the bank and do the 20 minute errand in either order. I could not do the 40 minute errand first as the bank would close. So the 40 minute errand is not a good choice for the first task.

Case 3: The bank closes at 6 (or later). Now it is possible to do one errand and visit the bank, in any order, and then do the other errand.

As you can see, visiting the bank first is bad in case 1, and doing the 40 minute errand is bad in case 2. Doing the 20 minute errand first is sensible in all of the cases. Therefore, doing the 20 minute errand is at least as good, or better, than doing anything else first and is a dominant strategy.

Once a dominant strategy is identified, the decision-making process is simple: you should play the dominant strategy.

In this example the closing time of the bank was an important variable in identifying the dominant strategy. The specification of the closing times itself reveals another example of game theory called *focal points*.

Focal Points (Schelling Points)

When I saw the time was 5:02pm, I was worried the bank might not be open. Why was that?

Notice that in theory banks can close at any time they wish. If they choose to close at 5:03pm every day, then they are legally allowed to do so.

But there is something very strange about picking a closing time like

5:03pm. Employees would be annoyed at having to stay 3 minutes past the hour, and customers might be confused as to why a bank would pick an unusual number.

It is customary and more natural for banks to close at a "round" time, like 5:00, 5:30, or 6:00.

These closing times are examples of the game theory concept of a *focal point*, also referred to as a Schelling point in honor of the economist Thomas Schelling who described them.

A *focal point* is a time or strategy that is natural or special in some way. Focal points are important because they allow people to coordinate without communication.

In the classic example by Thomas Schelling, people in an experiment were told they were to meet a stranger in New York City. Where would they choose to meet? Overwhelmingly people chose to meet at the Grand Central train station at noon—they would try to pick a prominent spot at a special time to increase the odds of meeting.

To return to the problem at hand, the concept of focal points allows us to infer the bank would close at a round time, such as 5:00, 5:30, or 6:00. You may say you know this by experience, but deep down that psychological reason has a strategic element to it.

The interesting part of focal points is that they help us coordinate. Let us now explore a few more classic examples of focal points.

Focal Points (Schelling Points)

Let's do a brief experiment. For the following seven tasks, your goal is to answer so as to match a partner who is separately answering the same questions. What would you pick?

1. Pick one: 'heads' or 'tails.'

2. Pick a number from the list: 7, 13, 99, 100, 261, 555.

3. We are to meet in a city but we cannot communicate in advance. Which of the following cities would you choose to have the highest chance of meeting me: Rome, Berlin, Paris, New York, London?

4. We have agreed to meet on a specific date, but the time was left unspecified and we cannot communicate. We have to meet at an exact minute. Which time will you choose?

5. Write a positive number.

6. Name an amount of money.

7. You are given 100 dollars to split into piles A and B. If your split of piles A and B matches your partner's, you get the amount in pile A and your partner gets the amount in pile B. How will you split up the money?

What Is The Purpose Of The Quiz?

These seven questions have a common theme: the goal in each is to coordinate the outcome without communicating. Situations like this are more generally called *coordination games*, where the strategy is to match what the other party is doing.

Questions similar to those above were asked to a group of 199 people with different cultural backgrounds. Here are the results that indicate some choices were more "obvious" and popular.

Results

1. *Pick one: 'heads' or 'tails.'* The common answer was 'heads', chosen by 69 percent of the people in the group.

2. *Pick a number from the list: 7, 13, 99, 100, 261, 555.* The common answer was 7, chosen by 36% of the people. This was followed by 100 (17%), 13 (14%), 261 (11%), 99 (13%), and 555 (9%).

3. *We are to meet in a city but we cannot communicate in advance. Which of the following cities would you choose to have the highest change of meeting me: Rome, Berlin, Paris, New York, London?* The top answers were nearly evenly divided between Paris (27%) and London (26%).

4. *We have agreed to meet on a specific date, but the time was left unspecified and we cannot communicate. We have to meet at an exact minute. Which time will you choose?* The most common answer was 12 noon (30%). The next most common answer of 2pm had only 6%.

5. *Write a positive number.* The most common answer was 7 (16%), followed by 2 (14%). It seems there was not too much consensus on this question.

6. *Name an amount of money.* The top answer of 1 million was chosen by 30% of people, followed by 100 with 11%.

7. *You are given 100 dollars to split into piles A and B. If your split of piles A and B matches your partner's, you get the amount in pile A and your partner gets the amount in pile B. How will you split up the money?* The answer of splitting the piles into 50/50 was given by 80% of people.

Coordination

Although these questions can be answered in a number of different ways, it turned out that many people gave the same answers. This is an example of how certain choices are more "natural" and their existence can help people coordinate in the lack of communication. In the next section, we give an application of focal points to public safety.

Source

Abitbol, Pablo. "An Experiment on Intercultural Tacit Coordination - Preliminary Report." MRPA paper. October 2009. http://mpra.ub.uni-muenchen.de/23474/1/MPRA_paper_23474.pdf.

The Game Of Bicycle Collisions

Bike safety is a big topic. Wear a helmet. Follow traffic laws, like halting at stop signs. Do not go too fast, and make sure your brakes work.

This is all useful advice. It has been beaten over my head since elementary school. Nonetheless, it did not help me from getting into bike accidents during college. To tackle that problem, I took advice that depended on game theory and the concept of focal points.

The Bike Game

Avoiding bike crashes is type of coordination game. Bikers want to coordinate to avoid occupying the same real estate at the same time. Consider a game of two bikers moving in opposing directions.

Imagine each biker has a choice of going straight, moving to his left, or moving to his right. Crashes occur when both bikers choose straight or they both swerve towards each other on either the left or right sides.

The remaining combinations, say one goes straight and other swerves right, will result in a safe exchange. There are three "crash" cases compared to six "safe" cases as depicted in the following figures.

Three "crash" cases

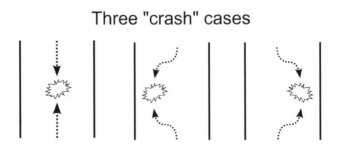

Six "safe" cases

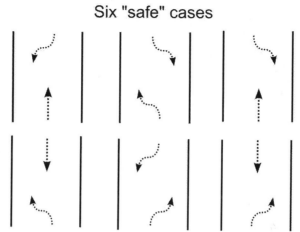

Thanks to the nature of the game, by random chance, it is twice as likely that the bikers will avoid each other rather than crash. Furthermore, there is a focal point that can reduce crashes. We Americans drive on the right hand side of the road, so it is natural that both bikers would swerve to their respective right sides.

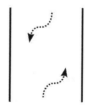

This rule of thumb helps avoid crashes. Plus, it doubles as a good tip for walking in hallways of American offices.

Unfortunately, our friendly human nature tends to undermine the safe focal point. What many of us do is get nervous and try to make eye contact with the other biker. When you make eye contact, you feel the need to mirror what the other person is doing. Because you have limited time to respond, you do not react fast enough. You even ruin the random chance of a safe passage and make crash the likely course.

And that is why the best advice I ever got about bike safety was this rule: *avoid eye contact with an oncoming biker*. It is not mind-blowing advice, nor does it always seem nice, but it is very practical. When you do not stare at the other person, you both will rely on the focal point of swerving to the right.

(My friends and I joked in college that the "no stare" advice is virtually impossible to follow when the oncoming biker is attractive. But then the game is different, as you probably wouldn't mind bumping into that person and starting up a conversation).

Some Students Make The Game More Difficult

As I mentioned earlier, focal points are dependent on culture. While avoiding eye contact gets to the "swerve right" equilibrium for Americans, it fails for many international students who drive on the left side of the road, and have the instinct to "swerve left."

Then, there is another twist. Some bikers aren't playing the game of coordination. They view the interaction more like a game of chicken. These people will never swerve because they do not want to slow down and often they enjoy the opportunity to yell at others.

The game is even more complicated since there are more variables. The realistic situation involves four-way intersections with high traffic. Now each biker has to coordinate with more than one other biker, and there are more bikers on the road. Even if natural bike safety reduced the crash rate to one percent, an intersection with 1,000 such games played per day would have about 10 crashes, which is quite a lot.

What can be done? Well, think back to the idea of focal points. A designer that hopes to increase the odds of success could nudge bikers into the right direction by *creating a focal point*. The implication is the bike game can be improved with better design.

Here is one implementation: create a bike circle with arrows to indicate the flow of one-way traffic.

If enough bikers follow the rules, then traffic will flow in one-way. Enforcement should come naturally. New bikers will also follow the traffic as that will be the safest route.

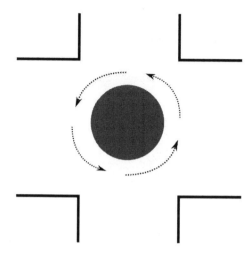

For its part, Stanford University did implement a traffic circle in a busy spot near the Quad that was called the "Intersection of Death." It is not clear if the number of accidents has gone down, as the same spot is now called the "Circle of Death."

Splitting A Soda Evenly

Continuing with the theme of coordination, I want to offer a story about sharing with siblings.

I have to thank my fifth grade math teacher for the story, which unintentionally introduced me to game theory. The game theory is hidden in the following extra-credit problem that he asked us.

> My mother would often give a can of soda to me and my two brothers and tell us to split it. Naturally, we all wanted more soda, but our Mom told us to be fair and split it—without arguing. After we failed, she came upon a solution that suited all of us. What method did we use to split the soda?

Most of us in the class thought mathematically and submitted answers about pouring 1/3 of the volume into each glass. My teacher told us these answers were incomplete because they described an outcome but not *how* the outcome would be achieved. Who would pour the soda? And what order do people pick? And how do you make everyone in the group trust each other?

Here is the solution the mom devised: one person was chosen to do the pouring. After the soda can was empty, the person who did the pouring would be the last to choose his glass. The method proved to be successful —the soda was always split evenly.

Why does the method work? It is because the method gives the person pouring an incentive to make the glasses as even as possible. If he does not pour the soda evenly, he will suffer because the other brothers pick the fuller glasses first. Another way of thinking about the solution is that the other brothers are made to trust the person pouring. And this is a remarkable trait because the brothers' interests are diametrically opposed.

This problem is example of *mechanism design*, which is the study of creating rules and incentives to allocate resources in what the designer sees as an efficient or fair way. Mechanism design is the theoretical basis to make markets work when they are not perfect, but it also comes up in many situations, like how airlines creatively price tickets.

The theory of mechanism design can also be used for your personal finances. I'm going to explain a motivational example based on the following simple question.

How Should You Split Your Paycheck?

How do you answer this question? Or in other words, what is your mechanism for achieving good financial outcomes?

Unless you plan, you are likely to use a greedy mechanism in which you use all of your paycheck (or even go into debt) for instant gratification. You will not have savings for expected purchases, like a down payment on a house, or for retirement.

If you are unhappy with your outcomes, why not change the design of your mechanism? Just as the three boys were made to split the soda evenly, you can create a mechanism to improve your finances.

In this example, it is instructive to think about yourself as three distinct people: the *inner child* of instant gratification, the *inner teenager* who can think at most five years into the future, and the *inner adult* who wants to have money during retirement. And think about your paycheck as the proverbial soda that your three "selves" need to split up.

Now it is very clear why people fail without planning: they satisfy only the inner child and leave nothing for the future selves. Their strategy is the equivalent of letting the person who pours the soda be the first one to pick.

Take a lesson from the soda mechanism: the person who chooses last needs to be the person pouring. Your retirement self is the one who is picking last, and by analogy, that is the person who should decide how to divide the check. An example might be to deduct 10% for retirement, 10% for the medium term, and the rest for current expenses. This strategy is commonly known as "paying yourself first," but you are really "paying your later self first," like a game theorist might.

How Game Theory Solved A Religious Mystery

While we are on the topic of debt and fair division, consider the following situation. A man owes debts of 100, 200, and 300, but dies with insufficient funds to pay everyone. How should his estate be divided?

As we all know, there might not be one correct answer. Fair division is a concept that depends as much on logic as it does on social custom. To see why, consider the following three situations that afford very different solutions.

1. A parent promises gifts to his children, but has to back off when a bonus is smaller than expected.

2. A publicly traded company issues shares of stocks and bonds, but soon goes bankrupt in an accounting scandal.

3. Partygoers order items at a restaurant, with promises to pay, and then end up arguing over the best way to split the bill.

There is not a single right way to approach any of these problems. That's what family fights, lawsuits, and restaurant arguments demonstrate every day. The conflict is a matter of perspective.

Some people prefer proportional division that depends on debt size. An example is the classic "pay what you ordered" method in restaurants where guests put money based on food they ordered. As logical as this sounds, not everyone desires this method.

Others prefer splitting things up equally. They argue it is the person—not the debt size—that matters. Equal division is a method for dividing gifts to children. During Christmas or holiday time, parents may choose to give every child the same gift size regardless of age or behavior.

What gets accepted depends on social custom. Getting everyone to agree is an exercise in persuasion, not in economics. It is possible for emotionally pleasing methods to beat more logically consistent systems.

One of the earliest discussions of fair division comes from the

Babylonian Talmud, a record of discussions about Jewish laws and customs. The Talmud contains a bankruptcy problem in the context of a man offering debts to his wives in excess of his assets. The Talmud answer is not immediately obvious, and in fact, the answer baffled academics for over almost 2,000 years. Let's see why.

The Talmud Answer

How should an estate be divided among three creditors claiming sums of 100, 200, and 300?

The Talmud offers answers through three examples. The text does not contain a general rule, which is what makes these answers seemingly contradictory. The three cases are when the estate size is 100, 200, and 300.

In the first case when the estate size is 100, the Talmud awards 33 1/3 to each party. The division suggests a principle of an equal division, which is easy mathematically and holds social appeal. But strangely this is not the same idea used in the other cases.

In the third case of 300, the Talmud offers a division of 50, 100, and 150. The math here is a proportional division based on the size of the debt. In modern times, proportional division holds wide appeal among lawyers and economists. But in this example, the puzzle is why is the 300 case treated differently than the 100 case?

If that question bothers you, then get ready for another surprise in the division for 200. In this case, the estate is supposed to be divided as 50, 75, and 75. Not only does the division not classify as an equal division nor a proportional division, but it is simply a curious decision altogether. Why should the second and third creditors be given the same amount of money? And where do the numbers come from?

Before I proceed, it is worth summarizing the claims in a table. We can think about the Talmud answers as a table that illustrates how an estate would be divided.

I provide an illustration below, in which the rows are estate sizes, the columns are claims, and the table entries are the division size.

		claims			
		100	200	300	
estate size	100	$33\frac{1}{3}$	$33\frac{1}{3}$	$33\frac{1}{3}$	equal division
	200	50	75	75	??? division
	300	50	100	150	proportional division

The division defied a proper explanation for almost 2,000 years, filling volumes of critical review. Some scholars had essentially given up and suggested the 200 case might be an issue of faulty transcription. And this is the unlikely background for which game theory enters and possibly saves the day.

Game Theory Offers An Answer

In the 1980s, Professors Robert Aumann and Michael Maschler wrote a paper claiming to have cracked the mystery.

They suggest there is no inconsistency in the Talmud answer. Aumann and Maschler demonstrate the Talmud answer can be viewed as a consistent application of a game theory principle. Why was game theory used? It turns out the Talmud answer is the solution (the nucleolus) of a properly defined coalitional game (sometimes called cooperative game theory). Aumann and Maschler explain the concept in lay terms as a single and consistent principle: equal division of the contested sum.

It is worth being skeptical before proceeding. Is the explanation simply a coincidence? After all, there are probably an infinite number of explanations that might produce the same split.

Aumann and Maschler justify their answer by examining other Talmudic passages and suggesting the same principle is applied in many topics. "Equal division of the contested sum" was apparently a social custom and that would help explain why it might seem strange to us but could have been natural for their culture.

Equal Division Of The Contested Sum

The Talmud examines a situation that might have been common to their times. Suppose two people are arguing over a garment. One claims half belongs to him while the other claims the whole is his. A judge is asked to decide who gets what. What would you do?

There are naturally various answers. One could propose an even split (1/2, 1/2) or a proportional split (1/3, 2/3).

But the Talmud offers a different answer, an answer that turns out to be an equal division of the contested sum (1/4, 3/4). How does this principle work? There are three stages. First, decide what portion of the cloth is being disputed. In this case, exactly half of the garment is being claimed by both parties. Second, split the disputed division among both parties—so 1/4 of the cloth is awarded to each. And third, give the remaining cloth—the "undisputed" portion—entirely to the person whose claim is not disputed.

This logic yields a split of 1/4 for the person claiming half of the garment and 3/4 for the person claiming the whole.

		claims	
		1/2	1
garment	1	1/4	3/4

This answer might seem strange, but remember that fair division methods depend on social custom.

The same method can be used for any problem among two parties, using the same three steps above.

1. Determine which portion is contested or claimed by both parties.

2. Split the contested portion equally.

3. Assign the uncontested portion to the sole person claiming it.

How else might this principle be applied? It can actually be applied to many situations, like when the claims are larger than the asset to be divided, as in the case of dividing an estate.

Equal Division Of The Contested Sum, Two Creditors

It is worth going through a few examples to get a feel for the idea. Let's examine how to divide estates of various sizes with two creditors claiming 100 and 300.

Example 1: (estate 66 2/3)

If the estate is 66 2/3, then the entire estate is contested. The split should be even at 33 1/3 going to each party.

Example 2: (estate 125)

If the estate is 125, then the first 100 is contested by both parties and divided evenly. The remaining 25 is entirely awarded to the 300-claimant. Hence, the division is 50 and 75.

Example 3: (estate 200)

Finally, if the estate is 200, then again the first 100 is contested by both parties and divided evenly. The remaining 100 is entirely awarded to the 300-claimant. Hence, the division is 50 and 150.

Here are the divisions in a table.

		claims	
		100	300
estate size	$66\frac{2}{3}$	$33\frac{1}{3}$	$33\frac{1}{3}$
	125	50	75
	200	50	150

Why stop there? Here are some examples when the claims are (100, 200) and (200, 300).

claims

	100	200
estate size 66 $\frac{2}{3}$	33 $\frac{1}{3}$	33 $\frac{1}{3}$
125	50	75
150	50	100

claims

	200	300
estate size 66 $\frac{2}{3}$	33 $\frac{1}{3}$	33 $\frac{1}{3}$
150	75	75
250	100	150

Explaining The Talmud Puzzle

Let's go back to the Talmud division for the three creditors. In the case of a 200 estate, the division was 50, 75, and 75 for parties that claimed debts of 100, 200, and 300.

To analyze this answer, let's do the following exercise. Take any two creditors and consider how they might split the total money awarded to them. Why would we do that? It is a check of *consistency*. It makes sense that pairs of creditors should have claims divided in a manner consistent with the way a disputed garment would be divided.

Consider the pair of creditors claiming 100 and 200. Together they are awarded a sum of 125. How is that sum split? It is split as 50 and 75. And amazingly, that matches the work we did in examples above: *this answer is consistent with an equal division of the contested sum!* The logic is that the first 100 is contested by both parties and split evenly, and the uncontested 25 is awarded to the 200-claimant.

In fact, the same observation can be seen when considering other pairs of creditors. Look at how much the 100 and 300 parties are getting. Together they receive a sum of 125, and this is split as 50 and 75. Again, *this answer is consistent with an equal division of the contested sum.*

Finally, consider the total reward to the 200 and 300 parties. In this case, the total sum of 150 is split as 75 to each. As the total sum is contested, this once again reflects an equal division of the contested sum.

In other words, when the mysterious Talmud solution is broken down by pairs of creditors, there is a consistent principle. I think this is quite remarkable.

Aumann and Maschler demonstrate the method can be extended, whether the claims are for three creditors, a hundred creditors, or even a million creditors. The same condition needs to be met: the assets are divided up such that *the amount received by any two people reflects the principle of equal division of the contested sum.* Furthermore, the division is a unique solution.

An Algorithm

It is good enough to see certain divisions are pairwise equal divisions of contested sums. But how do you find them starting from scratch? Aumann and Maschler show there is in fact only one division that is consistent. And this answer can be described by the following seven step algorithm.

1. Order the creditors from lowest to highest claims.

2. Divide the estate equally among all parties until the lowest creditor receives one half of the claim.

3. Divide the estate equally among all parties except the lowest creditor

until the next lowest creditor receives one half of the claim.

4. Proceed until each creditor has reached one-half of the original claim.

5. Now, work in reverse. Start giving the highest-claim money from the estate until the *loss*, the difference between the claim and the award, equals the loss for the next highest creditor.

6. Then divide the estate equally among the highest creditors until the loss of the highest creditors equals the loss of the next highest.

7. Continue until all money has been awarded.

Here is how the claims would be divided in the Talmud example.

		claims			
		100	200	300	
	50	$16\frac{2}{3}$	$16\frac{2}{3}$	$16\frac{2}{3}$	equal division
	100	$33\frac{1}{3}$	$33\frac{1}{3}$	$33\frac{1}{3}$	
	150	50	50	50	100 has $\frac{1}{2}$ of claim
	200	50	75	75	
	250	50	100	100	200 has $\frac{1}{2}$ of claim
estate	300	50	100	150	
size	350	50	100	200	loss is 100 to claims of 300 and 200
	400	50	125	225	
	450	50	150	250	loss is 50 to all claimants
	500	$66\frac{2}{3}$	$166\frac{2}{3}$	$266\frac{2}{3}$	
	550	$83\frac{1}{3}$	$183\frac{1}{3}$	$283\frac{1}{3}$	
	600	100	200	300	

Mystery solved? I think so. Not only do the Talmud answers follow a consistent principle, but they also rely on an idea that was mentioned as a custom. In that case, it is surely an interesting case that a tool of logic and rationality—game theory—was needed to decode the Talmud solution, which primarily depended on social custom.

Source

Journal of Economic Theory 36 (1985), pp. 195-213.

Coordination Failures

Focal points—choices that stand out and are attractive—are useful in coordination games because they help everyone make the same choice without communication. But it is not always the case that attractive choices are useful in all games. In competitive games, it is often the naturally appealing choice that creates conflict.

For instance, sports teams often compete for the same "star" player in bidding wars; journalists and news outlets seek to cover the most prominent story, often topping each other in coverage; bright students apply to the best ranked colleges, competing for limited seats; and commonly people seek to win the love of the most attractive mates, sometimes leading to vicious tactics.

In a coordination game, a naturally attractive option is a good thing. In a competitive game, each person seeks to be the winner, leading to a breakdown of cooperation.

The rest of this section will be devoted to covering competitive games in which individual interest is often at odds with group interest, leading to failures of coordination. We will provide several examples of how coordination failures arise in common examples. The first example is of a group of men hoping to win a date at a bar.

Nash Equilibrium

We jump right in with a stylized version of a bar scene. You and three male friends are at a bar trying to pick up women. Suddenly one blonde and four brunettes enter in a group. What's the individual strategy?

Here are the rules. Each of you wants to talk to the blonde. If more than one of you tries to talk to her, however, she will be put off and talk to no one. At that point it will also be too late to talk to a brunette, as no one likes being second choice. Assume anyone who starts out talking to a brunette has a good chance to succeed.

This scene is depicted in the move *A Beautiful Mind*, a Hollywood dramatization of the book of the same name about the game theorist John Nash. The blonde woman is like a focal point in that everyone finds her naturally the most attractive.

However, the fact that all of them want the blonde is a problem. If they all go for her, then at most one of them might succeed. Furthermore, the men will have ruined their chances for the night, as the brunettes will feel offended as no one likes to be second-choice.

What is the group to do? In the film, John Nash proposes a scheme to the group on how they should cooperate. He suggests, what if everyone goes for a brunette to start? Then each person has a high chance of succeeding, and everyone ends up with a good option.

So what do you think, is this a good plan? Let's analyze the situation strategically.

Definition: Nash Equilibrium

This is one of the most important concepts of game theory so it will be useful to take a break to define it and consider some examples.

A *Nash equilibrium* is a situation in which no person can improve his or her payout, *given what others are doing*. To put it another way, given the choices that everyone else is making, you are making the best possible choice that you can—the formal term, if you recall from Hotelling's game, is you are picking a *best response*.

Let's recap the concept of Nash equilibrium with some of the examples already covered in the book.

1) In Hotelling's game, the two hot dog stands sought the most customers. We analyzed that given where one hot dog stand was located, the other hot dog stand preferred to locate more centrally to win more customers. As each wishes to locate more centrally, they both end up preferring to be exactly in the center. At this point, neither could improve their profits, as that would mean locating non-centrally. That is why both locating in the center was a Nash equilibrium.

2) In the Bertrand Duopoly model, two firms compete solely on price. Each firm finds it profitable to undercut the other firm's price. The result is that each ends up picking the lowest possible price. At this point, neither firm can lower its price (as that would mean negative profits) nor can either firm raise its price (as that would lose all customers to the other firm). They are "stuck" into this outcome of a low price, and hence that is a Nash equilibrium.

As seen in these examples, a Nash equilibrium is not necessarily socially optimal (as we argued before, it would be better if the hot dog stands spread out on the beach), nor is it the best for the players in the game (firms in a Bertrand Duopoly game do not wish their prices were so low).

The point of a Nash equilibrium is that it is the result of competition when players take into account what others will do and how they can influence the game. Some Nash equilibria will seem fair while others will not.

However, when the Nash equilibrium is an undesirable outcome, we will not be fatalistic and pessimistic. We will explore in Section II techniques to *change the game*, which can bring players out of traps and bring about coordination.

For now, we will work on understanding the concept of a Nash equilibrium in more games. We must first understand why coordination failures happen and develop ideas on how to best fix them.

Go For The Blonde?

With the definition in mind, let us solve for the Nash equilibrium of the bar scene. When four guys are competing for brunettes and a single blonde, is it a smart strategy for everyone to go for a brunette?

We will answer this question by doing a small thought experiment. Let's suppose that everyone else in the group follows the plan, and your three friends agree to go for the brunettes. What is your best response? That is, what is the best thing you can do, given that they are going for the brunettes, and no one is going for the blonde?

You have two choices in this situation: you can either go for the brunette or the blonde. If you go for the brunette, you have a good shot at getting her. But then a thought creeps into your mind. With your friends going for brunettes, you have *no competition* if you go for the blonde. You realize that you now have a good shot at the blonde, and you thus would prefer to go for the blonde. So the answer is clear: if your friends go for the brunette, you should go for the blonde.

Now the question is, is this a Nash equilibrium? What we have to check is that no single person can do better given what everyone else is doing.

We already derived that you are playing a best response. It remains to check if your friends can do any better. Each of your friends has two choices: each can either stick with a brunette, or each can try talking to the blonde. But what happens if another person goes for the blonde? The stylized rules indicated that when two people go for the blonde—the friend and you—then both people would strike out. So clearly it is better for each of your friends to stick with their initial choice.

Therefore, we can conclude that you going for a blonde, and each friend going for a brunette, is a Nash equilibrium. Given what everyone has chosen, no one can do better.

(As a sidebar, the scene in the movie *A Beautiful Mind* does not actually depict a Nash equilibrium. John Nash proposes they all go for the brunettes, but then he has a flash of an idea and leaves the bar.)

This example also raises another point. In Hotelling's Game and the Bertrand Duopoly, each had a unique Nash equilibrium. In this bar game, as described, there are in fact several Nash equilibria. It was a Nash equilibrium when you went for the blonde, and everyone else went for the brunette. It is also a Nash equilibrium when exactly one person (not just you) goes for the blonde and everyone else goes for the brunette. The logic is symmetrical to the Nash equilibrium we just derived: when exactly one person goes for the blonde, obviously that person is playing a best response; additionally no other person can change from talking to a brunette to a better outcome.

So what is the actual strategy in this game, given that there are several Nash equilibria? This is a bit tricky, but we can take a hint from what happens in real life. Very likely each player is going to try to convince the others to go for the brunettes first so that he can go for the blonde.

Another complication is that in practical matters it will be hard to achieve the equilibrium that only one person goes for a blonde. There is going to be competition and someone in the group will probably sabotage the mission.

So there are several ways people use strategies outside of this stylized game. One strategy is to ignore the current group and wait for another group of blondes (the classic "wait and see" strategy). Another is to let a random group member go for the blonde as the others distract the brunettes (also practiced as "wingman theory").

But before taking the story too much to heart, remember this entire example treats the women extremely inaccurately and simplistically, in that they respond to what the men do. As we all know, dating is a game in which both sides can employ sophisticated strategies.

The point of this discussion is to remember that game theory is often about solving stylized and hypothetical games. The extent to which it can be applied depends on practical considerations. We will discuss much more of this in examples throughout this book.

Should You Buy Used Products?

Many financial articles praise used products, like "The Stuff I Never Buy Used" (Wisebread) or "Why First-Rate Folks Love Second-Hand Stuff" (MSN Money).

On face value, this advice is good because used products are usually cheaper. But how useful is the advice actually?

It is very, very important to think about advice critically in a game theory context. Recall in the bar scene from *A Beautiful Mind* the person who said "you should go for the brunette" really meant "I hope this sucker goes for the brunette so that I can go for the blonde." It turns out that the bar game might have an analogy in this situation of financial advice.

Let's run through a thought experiment to see why. Imagine you and all the readers of those articles actually follow the advice to buy used products. It is possible that as a consequence there is an increased demand for used products and a decreased demand for new products.

With enough demand, that would mean the price of used products would *rise*. Continuing with the logic, a sudden shift in demand would actually make used products relatively expensive, and consequently, new products would be relatively less expensive (both because demand dwindles and because those new products would have a better resale value, as buying used products becomes fashionable). In the extreme case, if the advice to buy used were actually adopted, it would actually make buying new the correct choice!

Now comes the kicker. The first people to recognize that new products are a good deal would be personal finance experts. And once this trend is clear, the same advisers would turn around and write articles advising you to buy new products, starting the cycle once again!

The overall point is that friendly financial advice has implications. The advice might be slightly good for you, but it is often better for the adviser. This is why you should be skeptical of personal finance advice, it is the reason I find a lot of advice insulting. So much of it is the equivalent of a friend telling me to go for the brunette while they go for the blonde.

The Prisoner's Dilemma

The Prisoner's Dilemma is arguably the most famous example of game theory. People have written entire books about it, such as William Poundstone's *The Prisoner's Dilemma* (1992). The game was developed at the RAND Institute in the 1950s. While the game has a tragic implication, the game helped popularize game theory because the story is captivating and it has many connections to common experience.

The classic version of the Prisoner's Dilemma is set at a police station. Two suspects are being questioned for a crime. While the police are pretty sure the suspects are guilty, they lack physical evidence and need at least one confession for a strong conviction.

The suspects are separated and interrogated in different rooms. The police do not use the usual tactics of bluffing to gain a confession. They instead tell each suspect that each will be rewarded or penalized based upon how each person acts. Here are the possible scenarios.

--If both suspects conceal information, then each will serve a 1 year sentence based on the minimal physical evidence.

--If both disclose information and confess, then both will be convicted and serve 3 years.

--If only one discloses information, then that suspect will be rewarded by being set free while the other partner will serve a heavier 4 year sentence as a penalty for not confessing.

What will be the outcome of this situation? At first glance, the suspects seem to be in a powerful situation. If both stay quiet, then the police have little evidence and they both serve a light sentence. This is the best joint outcome, and they are completely in control of their fates. But will it happen if each is thinking strategically?

At this point a diagram will help in illustrating the game.

Suspect 2

	Disclose	Conceal
Disclose	-3, -3	0, -4
Conceal	-4, 0	-1, -1

Suspect 1

The table summarizes the four possible outcomes based on whether each suspect conceals or discloses information (as each suspect has two choices, there are four outcomes in all). The two numbers in each cell indicate the payoff for each suspect as an ordered pair: (jail term for suspect 1, jail term for suspect 2). The numbers are negative to indicate the jail term is an undesirable outcome. This table is an example of a *game theory matrix*, and it will be used extensively throughout this book.

So what will happen in this game? Recall that a Nash equilibrium is about each person playing a best response to the other person. In other words, the way to approach the decision is to consider the best thing to do in response to each choice the other person might make. In this game, each suspect has to consider what is in his best interest when the other person discloses or conceals information.

Let's analyze each case by playing the role of a suspect. First, if the other suspect discloses information, what is the best thing for you to do? If you disclose information as well, then you face a sentence of 3 years. If, on the other hand you conceal information, then you will face a heavy sentence of 4 years. Clearly it is a best response to disclose if you know your partner is disclosing information by confessing.

Now, what is the best thing to do if your partner stays quiet and conceals information? In that case, you can either also conceal information, and face a 1 year sentence; or you can disclose information and cooperate with the police, in which case you will be set free. Again, it is better to disclose information.

You come to the conclusion that you should disclose information, as it is better for you regardless of what your partner does. In other words, you have concluded that disclosing information is a dominant strategy, and the lesson from before was that if you have a dominant strategy, then you should play it.

So you go ahead and disclose information. As it turns out, your partner also went through the same logic and also concluded that disclosing was a dominant strategy. Both of you disclose information to the crime and end up serving 3 years each.

The strange part is, if you had both simply stayed quiet (and ignored the dominant strategy), then you both would have only served 1 year each. In other words, by playing the best response, you both ended up in a worse outcome!

That in a nutshell is the dilemma that the prisoners face. When each person thinks about individual interest, the result is a Nash equilibrium that is worse for each in the group.

At this point there are a number of practical issues that might jump into your mind. First, it is not true in general that suspects always confess. Partly this is because they may fear being called a snitch and that comes with its own negative payoff (not modeled in this game). Second, if the suspects could communicate, then it might be possible that they both agree to stay quiet and avoid disclosing information. It is a key part of this game that the suspects are held separately exactly so they cannot communicate. Additionally, even if they agreed to work together, there is no contract that binds them to doing so. In a way, talk is cheap and one of the suspects might say he will stay quiet but then secretly change his mind and backstab the other.

The Prisoner's Dilemma is both tragic, in that the suspects could not cooperate, and delightful, in that the logic of each person was impeccable and the temptation to act selfish was almost unavoidable. The next few sections will illustrate several applications in everyday situations where the Prisoner's Dilemma affects how people act.

An Ancient Indian Proverb

While the Prisoner's Dilemma was formulated in the 1950s, the conflict between individual and group interest was well known since antiquity. There is an interesting example of the Prisoner's Dilemma in *A Collection of Telugu Proverbs* (Telugu is one of the languages spoken in India). The proverb must be hundreds of years old, as this book was published in 1868.

The proverb is "Cheating with sand, cheating with cowdung" and it refers to the following story.

Two travelers met and exchanged goods concealed in opaque bundles. One trader was offering raw rice in exchange for the other's parboiled rice. They agreed to the trade, and immediately ran off in different directions. But in the end, each found himself outwitted by the other. One trader ended up with sand instead of rice, and the other ended up with cow dung instead of parboiled rice.

This is a direct example of a Prisoner's Dilemma! To see why, consider the incentives of each trader.

--If you think the other trader will be honest, then it is more profitable to cheat and offer nothing than to honestly offer up your good.

--If you think the other trader will cheat you, then it is obvious you want to cheat in return, rather than giving up something for nothing.

Each trader has a dominant strategy to cheat and they do. But had they both played fairly, then they would have traded and actually ended up with the exchange they initially wanted.

The story is a warning that any bilateral transaction could possibly degenerate into a Prisoner's Dilemma if the parties do not trust each other. It's a testament to modern society and finance that a variety of mechanisms (like reputation and punishment) can generate cooperation and trust.

Left to fend for ourselves, we might never accomplish anything. As the Spanish proverb goes: "One trick is met by another."

Visiting The Doctor

"So take these pills, get a blood report, and see me in a few weeks," said my doctor. I was somewhat taken aback. It was my first physical as an adult. I was healthy overall, but I was being advised to take a prescription drug as a precaution that possibly would be needed for the rest of my life. I was not sure what to do. Could I trust my doctor?

Generally doctors can be trusted and are good people. However, patients may be skeptical about the necessity of drug prescriptions, tests, and surgeries, because American health care tends to pay for activity instead of health outcomes. The issue of trust can become a Prisoner's Dilemma.

The Medical Consultation Game

Consider an obese adult who requires but does not want medical attention. At the request of friends, he visits a doctor.

The doctor has two choices when he meets with the patient. Suppose he can choose whether to spend 5 minutes to prescribe mildly effective medicines or he can spend 15 minutes and describe more effective lifestyle changes to diet and exercise (extra effort).

The adult also has two choices when he meets the doctor. He can either choose to ignore the advice and get a second opinion, or he follow the doctor's recommendation (extra effort).

There are four possible outcomes from these choices.

--Both put in the extra effort: doctor gives lifestyle advice and patient complies. This is the best outcome for both.

--Only the doctor puts in the extra effort: doctor gives lifestyle advice and patient ignores it.

--Only the patient puts in the extra effort: doctor gives medicine and patient takes it.

--Neither one puts in the extra effort: doctor gives medicine and patient does not take it.

The best outcome is that both put in the extra effort. But how might each think about the situation strategically?

Unfortunately, the payoffs resemble the Prisoner's Dilemma and both the doctor and the patient are more likely to avoid putting in the extra effort. Here is why.

The patient thinks about whether to ignore the advice and possibly seek a second opinion. If the doctor prescribes ineffective medicine, the patient is better off ignoring the advice. If the doctor gives the good advice on lifestyle, then the patient is still tempted to ignore it, as the patient can always seek corroboration with a second opinion.

The doctor's perspective can be somewhat similar. Knowing the patient will ignore the advice, the doctor is better off dispensing medicine quickly as at least the doctor uses less time. Suspecting the patient will follow the advice, the doctor is still tempted to prescribe medicine, as in general there is a belief that patients do not change their lifestyle but might take their prescriptions.

In the end, it is a dominant strategy for neither party to put forth extra effort. The result is that doctors write prescriptions and patients do not take them or they get a second opinion. So in spite of the possible gains, the best outcome where both cooperate cannot be achieved.

The bad news is this outcome is not too much of a stretch from what commonly happens in a medical consultation. The good news is that the situation is a model, and not all doctors and patients behave this way. Some doctors are great and will make the extra effort, as will some patients. There is also a potential gain where patients can learn to trust their doctors, and that will make both more likely to put in the extra effort.

The issue of trust is important, and even in the medical room the Prisoner's Dilemma influences outcomes.

Source

The above story was adapted from a 2004 issue of *Quality and Safety in Health Care* called "Models of the medical consultation: opportunities and limitations of a game theory perspective" by C. Tarrant, T. Stokes, and A. M. Colman.

Prisoner's Dilemma At The Casino

My friend Jamie is a professional poker player, and he is used to analyzing problems strategically. Once while he was in Las Vegas, he noticed a bit of game theory in the entry rules.

Jamie was registering for a tournament at Caesar's Palace. The tournament rules specified a $65 entry fee that came with 2,500 chips. But there was an option to buy an additional 500 chips for $5 more. Should he buy the extra chips?

Jamie did a quick mental calculation. The initial buy-in values translated to 2.5 cents per chips, whereas the optional buy-in translated to getting chips at the rate of 1 cent per chip. This made the optional buy-in a no-brainer and Jamie bought the chips.

But there was a catch. The optional buy-in *did not add to the prize pool of the tournament*. The optional buy-in went directly to the casino. This detail made the game a multi-person Prisoner's Dilemma.

Why is that? Think about the decision to buy extra chips. Each individual player thinks as follows: if the other players do not buy the extra chips, then it is certainly a good idea to buy the extra chips at a bargain price. Having extra chips at a poker table (being the "big stack") can be a huge advantage in terms of betting power. What if the other players buy the extra chips? Well, then it is again a no-brainer: the extra buy-in is needed just to stay even with the other players.

In the end, every poker player finds it a dominant strategy to buy the extra chips. The problem is that all the extra money goes directly to the casino, not the prize pool. Thus, when everyone does the optional $5 buy-in, everyone starts out with the same size stack of 3,000 chips, but the prize pool remains the same. The net effect is everyone has paid $5 extra to compete for the same amount of prize pool money.

This is a remarkable example of the Prisoner's Dilemma. Jamie bought the extra chips, and I have no doubt I would do the same. Jamie hears that most casinos in Las Vegas have a similar policy of optional buy-ins. And that would make sense, as it is a smart move for the casino.

JC Penney Loses $163 Million

JC Penney wanted to change the game. The large retailer felt customers were sick of complicated clearance sales and annoying pricing tricks. In 2012, JC Penney launched a simplified pricing scheme with predictable low prices every day. They even used whole numbers like selling a shirt for $7 instead of $6.99.

The move was considered a big risk, and it turned out the gamble did not pay off. In 2011, JC Penney made $64 million in the first quarter. In 2012, just one year later, it lost $163 million in the first quarter.

What went wrong? I think partly this can be understood as an example of the Prisoner's Dilemma.

Honesty Versus Trickery

There is nothing inherently wrong with JC Penney's pricing. In fact, I'd say honest pricing is a refreshing change from the standard nickel and dime tactics of most stores.

The problem, however, was the context of its strategic move. The problem was that *other* companies did not adopt honest pricing.

To illustrate why, consider the following game. Imagine two companies who can either choose to use "honest" pricing or "tricky" pricing. Suppose the game has the following characteristics:

--The marketplace is worth 100 units of profit.

--It costs money and resources (10 units) to play "tricky" pricing.

--If both play "honest" or "tricky", each splits the market profits.

--If one company is "honest" and the other "tricky," the tricky company gets nearly all the market (nets 80) against the few that stick with honest pricing (10).

Here are the net payoffs to the game.

Store 2

		Honest	Tricky
Store 1	Honest	50, 50	10, 80
	Tricky	80, 10	40, 40

One thing you will notice is this: if both companies play "honest," the total value of the marketplace is 100.

If they both play "tricky," however, then each loses 10 units for the cost of constantly running promotions. So they both only get 40 units and the market is only worth 80 units in all.

The same deadweight loss happens when one company is "honest" and another is "tricky." The "honest" company gets 10, but the "tricky" gets a net 80 so the total marketplace is worth 90—with 10 units lost for the cost of being "tricky." How does this game play out?

The Prisoner's Dilemma Of Honest Pricing

In theory, both could realize the destructive nature of running "tricky" pricing: they each have to waste 10 units to run the promotions which are a net waste for society.

If both played the "honest" strategy, then each would get 50 each. But what is the strategy to the game? Here is how a company might think.

--If the other company plays "honest," then I can either get 50 units for playing "honest," or I can get 80 units for playing "tricky." Clearly it is better to play "tricky."

--If the other company plays "tricky," then I can either get 10 units for playing "honest," or I can get 40 units for playing "tricky." Again, it is better to play "tricky."

The conclusion is clear: it is best to play a "tricky" pricing strategy in this game, regardless of what the other company does!

A nice article from MSNBC quotes behavioral economist Xavier Gabaix on why fair pricing was not a good idea: "Once you educate consumers on the right way to shop, they will seek out the lowest cost store, and that will be the one with the shrouded prices. Once they are savvier consumers, you make less money from them."

This problem is analogous to the Prisoner's Dilemma: both companies could benefit if they played honestly, but instead they are tempted to discount and steal customers from the other company.

The result is an equilibrium of discounting and lots of time spent shopping for discounts. And that is probably a bad thing for everyone, JC Penney and consumers alike.

Source

Sullivan, Bob. "NBC News Technology." *NBC News*. 25 May 2012. Web. http://www.nbcnews.com/business/consumer/fair-square-pricing-thatll-never-work-jc-penney-we-being-f794530.

Unbranding

So far we have been discussing the Prisoner's Dilemma and how it is bad for the players. This example will be a twist in which there will be a beneficiary from the incentives.

A celebrity endorsement is usually a win-win: the company increases visibility for its product, and the celebrity gets paid in compensation. But things get trickier when the celebrity has a controversial or trashy image: the company may want to distance itself, but it also does not wish to alienate the celebrity's fans either.

Jersey Shore was a short-lived reality TV show on MTV from 2009 to 2012. The premise of the show was to have Americans of Italian heritage party in the summertime at the Jersey Shore. The show was tremendously popular and it received record ratings for MTV. The partying on the show was wild, and often members of the cast were shown partying too hard.

One example was Nicole Polizzi, nicknamed "Snooki," who was often shown vomiting in designer handbags like Gucci and Coach. Evidently the handbag companies were worried the negative publicity might tarnish their reputations. And so they started playing a little game, by means of "unbranding."

Snooki was allegedly receiving handbags from both Gucci and Coach. But NBC Philadelphia reported there was a twist in this paid celebrity endorsement: "The kicker: Coach is not sending [Snooki] Coach bags. They're sending her Gucci bags, and any other competing designer product they can..."

And yet, it is funny how each company was fighting by trying to destroy the competitor. They were probably thinking along the logic in terms like "the enemy of my enemy is my friend." But on closer analysis, the game is not good for the companies. In fact, **this type of brand warfare is a Prisoner's Dilemma**.

Why is that? Think about the game between Coach and Gucci. Each company has the choice of sending nothing, or spending money to hurt the competitor. How will each play the game? It is pretty easy to see the dominant strategy is for each to try and backstab the other. If the other company is backstabbing by sending your handbags, you will retaliate by sending their handbags. And if the other company does nothing, all the more reason to try and unbrand your company by sending Snooki a competitor handbag.

In the end, both companies end up sending Snooki a designer handbag of the other company. But because they both do this, both of their images get hurt anyway, and they have spent money to participate.

In spite of the seemingly clever strategies, the companies are the clear losers of this unbranding game. And the winner of the game is...Snooki! It is not often when a negative image leads to getting free designer handbags. But that is the power of the Prisoner's Dilemma: if you can get *others* to play it, *you* can end up a winner.

Source

Masterson, Teresa. "No Backsies! Designers Unload Competitors' Swag on Snooki." *NBC 10 Philadelphia*. NBCUniversal Media, 20 Aug. 2010. Web. http://www.nbcphiladelphia.com/news/local/No-Backsies-Designers-Unload-Competitors-Swag-on-Snooki-101166409.html.

The Competitive Edge

I'm going to shift gears from the TV show *Jersey Shore* to the esteemed periodical *The Economist* (I bet no one has written that sentence before!). But there is a connection between Snooki's accidental winning strategy and *The Economist's* subscription promotion strategy as the Prisoner's Dilemma applies to both.

I like reading *The Economist* and occasionally the magazine will contain promotional inserts to encourage gift subscriptions for students. The ad copy tends to focus on how the magazine offers "world-class insights" that "inform and inspire." But one of the ads I saw was a bit more interesting from a strategic perspective.

The text of the ad is "Give the student the competitive edge with a gift subscription to *The Economist*."

It was the specific phrase "competitive edge" that caught my attention. It struck me as a clever way that *The Economist's* framing the game of subscribing as a Prisoner's Dilemma–with the magazine as the winner. Let's think about the game to understand why.

What Is Good Trivia?

Consider the question, "What is the first song that played on MTV?" As far as trivia goes, this has all the makings of a good question. It's about an interesting moment in TV history and the answer is also fitting–"Video Killed the Radio Star."

But there's just one glaring issue with this potential question: *everyone knows this is the answer* and that makes it fairly useless trivia. People who smugly bring up the fact are not seen as smart; they are quietly mocked for not realizing that everyone else already knows it.

The point of this story is that sometimes knowledge can be a competitive good. To have an edge and win in trivia, you can't just answer things everyone else knows. You have to know something and hope that other people don't know it. And that brings us back to the claim made by *The Economist*.

The Prisoner's Dilemma Of Reading

What is the benefit to subscribing to *The Economist?* One perspective is to consider individual gain. In that decision, you only need to judge whether the magazine provides value in excess of its subscription cost.

But you can also evaluate the decision in terms of gaining a competitive edge. In that case, you have to think about the decisions of other people. That is where game theory comes into play.

Consider the game where you choose "read" or "don't read" the magazine. Other people are making the same decision. The payoff will depend on the actions that both parties choose. Here are the possible scenarios that can take place:

--Neither party reads and they stay in the status quo (a payoff of 0 to each).

--One party reads and the other doesn't. The party that reads gets a competitive edge (a payoff of +1) and the party that doesn't is at a competitive disadvantage (a payoff of -2).

--Both parties read. In this case there is no "edge" since both parties learn the same knowledge. Furthermore, both parties incur costs of the magazine subscription fee and the time expended to read. The net result is that both parties are worse off than if neither had read (a payoff of -1).

Here is a game matrix of the payouts.

Others

		Read	Don't
You	Read	-1, -1	1, -2
	Don't	-2, 1	0, 0

What is the strategy in this game? Imagine how each party thinks.

If the other party doesn't read the magazine, then it will be better to read (+1) than to not read and stay in the status quo (0). On the other hand, if the other party *does* read the magazine, then it becomes a game of not being left behind. You would rather expend energy and effort to read the issue (-1) instead of being lazy and falling into a competitive disadvantage (-2).

Both parties see that reading is a dominant strategy, and they both end up subscribing to *The Economist.* In the end, both end up worse off than the status quo as they spend money and time just to make sure the other does not gain a competitive edge.

The winner of the game is *The Economist* which gained a couple of new subscriptions!

Caveats

The analysis above is strictly limited to the question of whether reading a highly circulated magazine could provide a competitive advantage. There are, of course, other ways to read the news—for free or at a low cost—which have definitely hurt magazine subscriptions. And just because someone subscribes to a magazine does not mean the person reads it or understands it. It is possible for both parties to gain as well, if one person benefits from the political articles while another person benefits from the business articles.

Finally, knowledge can be mutually beneficial too. It's a good thing when society becomes more educated and people think more critically. Plus, on a personal note, it's fun to talk to people who read interesting books or magazines. The students might lose the Prisoner's Dilemma of gaining a competitive edge, but it seems they, and society, can win in the long-run.

Southwest Airlines Makes $144 Million

A pattern is emerging from the past few examples. My friend Jamie and the retailer JC Penney both lost money when participating in a Prisoner's Dilemma. It is generally bad to be a player in a Prisoner's Dilemma as selfish motives, and dominant strategies, lead to a destructive outcome for the group. On the other hand, Snooki accidentally engaged Coach and Gucci in a Prisoner's Dilemma and she benefited tremendously. Similarly, *The Economist* advertising is enticing new readers to play Prisoner's Dilemma, hoping to increase subscriptions. The general lesson is that you do not want to play the Prisoner's Dilemma. What you want to do is create a situation where others have to play it and you can profit. The players' loss can be your gain. This is a very important business lesson that will be illustrated in this section.

Southwest Airlines is unique in its boarding process. Rather than providing assigned seats, Southwest has a policy of "open-seating." This means that during the boarding process travelers are free to sit in any available seats.

As an aside, people have a love/hate relationship with open-seating. The bad part is that groups and families cannot reserve seats and might get split up. The good part is that open-seating is much faster than assigned seating. Shorter times at the gate save Southwest money, and that indirectly keeps airfares low.

The cost savings are a major reason Southwest has employed open-seating for its entire 42-year history. Since 2007, however, there have been a couple of notable changes.

One change, in particular, translated into revenue of $98 million in 2010 and $144 million in 2011. And, as I'll explain below, the revenue is a consequence of pitting customers into a Prisoner's Dilemma game.

Recent Changes To Open Seating

While Southwest does not assign individual seats, it does have an organized procedure for how passengers board the aircraft.

Prior to 2007, passengers generally boarded on a first-come, first-serve basis. That is, travelers who arrived at the gate earliest could board first and pick the most favorable seats. This lead to passengers "camping out" at the gate to secure a good boarding position and it was accompanied by minor arguments as people tried to save seats or cut in line.

In 2007 Southwest decided to end this "cattle call" process. The new process assigned each traveler a boarding group A, B, or C and boarding number. Travelers in group A went first, then B, and then C. Within each group, a traveler with a lower boarding number got on the airplane first. Travelers could still choose seats once on board the airplane, but there was much less chaos at the gate because people could line up in a specified order.

How were travelers assigned a boarding number? The number was based on the time at which the traveler checked in for the flight. Someone who checked in at the earliest time, 24 hours in advance of the flight, could secure a favorable boarding assignment. A traveler who forgot to check in online was often doomed and would have to wait at the end of the line.

The boarding assignment changed the game in a very interesting way. Instead of rewarding passengers who waited at the gate the longest (people who did not value their time), the boarding assignment generally rewarded people who could check in online in advance (people who were organized and generally well-off).

A secondary market sprung up to capitalize on the technology of online-boarding, with some websites offering to automatically check a traveler in at the earliest time 24 hours before a flight. The service was reliable and cost $1, a very appealing offer for the busy business traveler.

These third-party websites were tolerated until Southwest shut them down and decided that it should be the one profiting. In 2009, Southwest unveiled the most recent change to open-boarding called EarlyBird Check-in. It was this option that lead to millions of dollars in extra fees.

The EarlyBird Prisoner's Dilemma

Southwest explained the EarlyBird Check-in in a press release, "Don't race. We'll save your place! Southwest is proud to announce its newest product, EarlyBird Check-in, which gives Customers the option to score an early boarding position by adding an additional $10 to the price of a one-way fare. The low-cost service automatically reserves a boarding position for Customers prior to general check-in..."

Instead of playing the seating lottery, customers who were willing to pay could secure priority seating by paying $10 per one-way flight. The nuance was that EarlyBird Check-in did not guarantee a good seat. It only meant the airline checked that traveler in automatically.

In many travel columns, people wondered if the service provided a good value. But on a larger level, those discussions missed the true nature of the situation. The genius is the EarlyBird Check-in threw travelers into a Prisoner's Dilemma from which Southwest could mightily profit!

Here is the game. An individual traveler wonders if he should pay $10 to be automatically checked-in for his flight. In his mind, the game is:

--Pay $10 for good seat.

--Pay $0 for a lottery style seating.

But the game is more complicated than that. In fact, the traveler is competing with others who are making exactly the same decision!

Consider the game between two travelers who compete for the best seat. The possible outcomes are:

--If neither pays for EarlyBird, then both can expect okay seats in the seating lottery.

--If only one pays $10 for EarlyBird, that person gets a good seat.

--If *both* pay $10 for EarlyBird, then they both get put into a lottery for priority seats. This essentially means they are competing in a seating lottery, but they both have to pay $10 to do it.

The game is like a Prisoner's Dilemma. If other traveler does not do EarlyBird Check-in, then someone who cares about a good seat will pay $10 for EarlyBird Check-in. If the other traveler does do EarlyBird Check-in, then buying EarlyBird Check-in is better than ending up with a bad seat for sure. Paying the $10 for EarlyBird Check-in is a dominant strategy!

The payoffs are presented in table form in the following figure.

Traveler B

		EarlyBird Check-in	Not
Traveler A	EarlyBird Check-In	A okay seat B okay seat	A good seat B bad seat
	Not	A bad seat B good seat	A okay seat B okay seat

In the end, both might be better served saving $10 and playing the seating lottery. But since they compete, they end up spending $10 for the privilege of playing a seating lottery.

The Bottom Line: Profits, Profits, Profits

Now there are some travelers who never will pay $10. But practically, a good portion are willing to pay for the privilege and are caught in this Prisoner's Dilemma.

Southwest has profited tremendously from EarlyBird Check-in. In 2010, Southwest reported an extra $98 million in revenue from EarlyBird Check-in, exceeding expectations. In 2011, Southwest revenue from EarlyBird Check-in grew 44 percent. The service translated to an extra $142 million in revenue.

Originally, few people paid for EarlyBird Check-in and that meant a guaranteed good seat. Now, so many people do pay that even Southwest admits paying for EarlyBird may not guarantee boarding within the first 60 positions, "While EarlyBird Check-In doesn't guarantee an A boarding position [that is, the first 60 positions], it improves your seat selection options to help you get your favorite seat."

The brilliant part is that travelers are essentially stuck in this game. Individual travelers cannot stop playing this game as it will result in bad seating. Furthermore, as more people pay for priority boarding, this sends the remaining travelers into worse and worse boarding positions. So the game essentially attracts more people to opt for EarlyBird Check-in.

Of course, there is a limiting factor to this game. If too many people opt for EarlyBird Check-in, then Southwest cannot guarantee all these travelers good seats. Some people will end up in bad boarding positions and will feel pissed off they paid for it, eroding the value of EarlyBird Check-in.

Still, this is unlikely to be a problem any time soon. Southwest is the airline of choice for cost-conscious travelers, so ultimately many travelers will never pay for this service and EarlyBird will still offer priority seating.

That means EarlyBird Check-in should be profitable for years to come. Well done, Southwest.

Sources

"2011 Southwest Airlines One Report." *Southwest Airlines*. Web. http://www.southwestonereport.com/2011/pdfs/2011SouthwestAirlinesOneReport.pdf.

Mutzabaugh, Ben. "Southwest's EarlyBird Check-in: Worth the $10?" *USATODAY.COM*. 2 Dec. 2012. Web. http://travel.usatoday.com/flights/post/2009/12/southwests-earlybird-check-in-worth-the-10-/620002946/1.

"Southwest Airlines Introduces EarlyBird Check-In, a New Customer." Bloomberg.com. Bloomberg, 2 Sept. 2009. Web. http://www.bloomberg.com/apps/news?pid=newsarchive&sid=apbcKiO6pb0s.

"You Spoke and We Listened - Southwest Airlines Says Open Seating is Here to Stay!" Southwest Airlines Investor Relations - News Releases. 18 Sept. 2007. Web. http://southwest.investorroom.com/index.php?s=43&item=1060.

Golden Balls TV Show

There is a British TV game show called *Golden Balls*. One of the segments in the show is a game called "Split or Steal." The game involves an amount of prize money (say £100,000). The prize money is divided depending on how each of two contestants chooses to "split" or "steal" the money. If both players "split," then they share the prize money equally. If one chooses "split" and the other "steal," then the person who chose "steal" gets everything and the other person gets nothing. If they both "steal," then both go home with nothing.

Person 2

		Split	Steal
	Split	50%, 50%	0%, 100%
Person 1	Steal	100%, 0%	0%, 0%

The game is a perfect example of the Prisoner's Dilemma. Each contestant has a dominant strategy of choosing the "steal" ball, but if they both do that, they both go home with nothing. But there is a twist to the game show in that both people are in the same room and they can talk to each other before choosing. Will this extra amount of communication help them?

In one episode that aired March 14, 2008, there was £100,150 of prize money up for grabs. Sarah and Stephen were discussing strategy. Stephen explained that he was going to split, as he felt everyone watching on TV would hate him if he stole. Sarah echoed this sentiment saying that she would split because her friend would be disgusted if she stole the money.

They made their final promises and then the host asked them to reveal their choices. Stephen unveiled his choice which was "split," and Sarah showed hers and it was....a "steal"! Sarah ended up winning the entire

£100,150.

Honestly it is a bit gut-wrenching to watch. Stephen tried his best, but ultimately he faced a no-win situation because Sarah could not overcome having been betrayed in a previous game. Sarah was clearly not playing the game at hand but instead considering a bigger game in which she wanted to avoid being double-crossed again.

It would have been nice to see them cooperate, but Sarah played the dominant strategy. The lesson is that even when you can communicate in a Prisoner's Dilemma, that still might not be enough as there is no way to enforce the agreement.

Source

Golden Balls. "£100,000 Split Or Steal? 14/03/08." Online video clip. YouTube. YouTube, 14 Mar. 2008. Web. 21 Sept. 2013. http://www.youtube.com/watch?v=p3Uos2fzIJ0

Beating The Prisoner's Dilemma

Most people approach the Prisoner's Dilemma as follows. They know
that the dominant, selfish strategy will be bad for the group, if everyone
plays it. So they usually try to convince people not to play their dominant
strategy. In the TV show *Golden Balls*, contestants are faced with a
choice to "split" or "steal" a share of prize money, and they usually
spend their time promising they will "split" and ask the other person to
do so as well.

But as the last example just illustrated, this is not a foolproof strategy,
nor is it a particularly good one. You should be careful about trusting the
other person in a Prisoner's Dilemma, and the other person should be
skeptical of your motives as well. Nevertheless, there is an ingenious
method of how a Prisoner's Dilemma can be defeated, as demonstrated in
another episode of *Golden Balls*.

Why Splitting Is A Bad Promise

First, I want to reiterate why the strategy of promising to split does not
work. When you promise the other person you will split the prize, you
are trying to change the game.

		Person 2	
		Split	Steal
Person 1	Split	50%, 50%	0%, 100%

You are telling another person that instead of looking at the original
payoffs, that person should only consider the game under the assumption
that you are going to split the prize. So you are telling the other person to
consider the following game.

Do you see what's wrong with your strategy? If you promise that you
will split the prize, the other person has the very tempting option to steal.
If that person splits, the prize is only 50 percent against the choice of
stealing which results in the entire 100 percent.

And therein lies the problem: if you promise you will SPLIT the prize, then you pretty much are telling the other person not to worry about the mutual steal option. This makes it a very good idea for the other person to STEAL the prize.

Clearly it is a bad idea to promise that you will split the prize. Is there another way out?

Know Thyself

There is a remarkably devious way to get cooperation: you must tell them that you will STEAL the prize!

How does this strategy play out? On one episode, the action proceeded as follows. One contestant, Nick, immediately announced, "I want you to trust me. 100 percent I am going to pick the steal ball. I want you to choose split, and I promise you that I will split the money with you [after the show]."

The other contestant was completely stunned by this strategy, and the audience found it amusing too.

The next two minutes were a funny exchange. Nick kept explaining why he was going to steal, and the other was dumbfounded by this threat. He wondered, why can't they both split? The host reminded them Nick's plan was risky, as there was no legal requirement for him to keep his promise to split the money once the show was over.

Nick was called an idiot by the other contestant who just could not believe his predicament. Nick had taken control of the game, and he did not act nice. Why should the other person cooperate? Nick promised over and over that he was an honest person and that he would definitely split the money after the show.

After the discussion, they revealed their choices. The other contestant followed through and revealed his choice of SPLIT. And then Nick's action turned out to be...SPLIT as well! They both ended up sharing 50 percent of the money evenly, but the other person wondered why Nick had to be sinister in claiming that he would steal. Couldn't he have just explained he would be nice too?

Here is why Nick's strategy was so brilliant. Nick was credibly explaining that he was going to steal. This changed the game into the following payoffs.

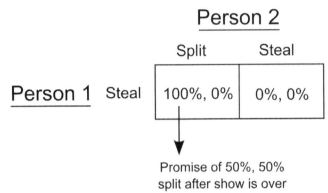

Promise of 50%, 50%
split after show is over

On the one hand, the other contestant could steal and destroy the prize money. On the other, he could split and hope that Nick kept to his word. In other words, Nick had transformed the game so that the weakly dominant strategy was to split!

The other contestant was happy at the outcome, but he shouted, "Why did you put me through that?" as he really had to struggle over his decision, only to learn Nick would cooperate after all.

I think Nick has shown a brilliant way to beat the Prisoner's Dilemma in a one-shot game. His statement that he would steal is a credible threat, and once assured the other person would split, he could then split and be generous. While this might not work if the game were repeated, or if the other player was angered by the threat, Nick has demonstrated a smart way to increase the chance of splitting the prize in a one-shot game.

Source

Golden Balls. "golden balls. the weirdest split or steal ever!" Online video clip. YouTube. YouTube, 3 Feb. 2012. Web. 21 Sept. 2013. http://www.youtube.com/watch?v=S0qjK3TWZE8

Section II: Changing the Game

The first part of this book was all about recognizing strategic situations and seeing how incentives led to particular outcomes. That would be all one needs to know about game theory, if all game theory concerned itself with was games played simultaneously, and only one time with fixed players, rules, and payoffs.

But real life situations involve more complicated games in which people might act in sequence as opposed to moving simultaneously, the game might be played more than once, and players might be able to change the rules and affect the outcome.

It is a common mistake to get angry at a bad outcome. But as the first section illustrates, it is often not the fault of the people playing the game. In Hotelling's game, Bertrand competition, and the Prisoner's Dilemma, the poor outcomes are not because the people playing the games are stupid: it is precisely because the players are thinking smartly!

So what should you do when things turn out poorly? The theme of this section is that if you do not like how a game turns out, then there is no need to get angry at how people acted. You should instead look for ways to *change the game*. This section will illustrate a number of ways to influence the outcome.

The Office Phone Problem

Here is some advice you can take to the office: if you aren't winning the game you are playing, consider changing the game.

If you find yourself yelling at people, please stop and think about why people are acting that way. Just asking people to change is hard. Rational people respond to incentives and act accordingly. To improve outcomes, it will often be better to change the game than to scold bad behavior.

Here is a story along those lines when my friend worked at a consulting job in a small office. Once, his office had a problem because the administrative staff could not handle all incoming phone calls. It looked terrible that calls from clients went to voicemail during normal business hours.

So a new system was put in place: calls from the main line would roll over to all entry-level employees after the first two rings. At the outset, the system seemed great because administrators would pick up most calls as usual, and the safety mechanism meant entry-level employees (an additional five people) were available to answer. And yet just two days after the installation, an important call was missed.

The resulting investigation was embarrassing. It turned out there were two entry-level employees who could have answered the phone. The administrator was furious and scolded them for not picking up the phones. Was it right to yell at them? As a game theorist, I point the finger back at the system, which created improper incentives.

Let's consider how an employee might react when the call rolls over. The person will probably use the following logic, "Well, I know the phone is ringing, but I don't want to be bothered now. After all, there are four other people who might pick up the phone. I think I'm going to wait and see if someone else might pick up."

This kind of logic is the result of two important (and dangerous) characteristics of the game.

1. There Are *Free Riders*

Free riders are people who get the benefits of a common good without contributing to the cause. In the phone game, the company only cares if the phones are answered, which makes the entire office look good. People who never answer the phones are free riders because they get the benefit of looking good without having to answer the calls.

2. Answering The Phone Becomes A *Game of Chicken*

The classic game of chicken involves two players driving at each other at high speeds. Players can either "swerve" or "maintain course." If both players swerve, they are both called chickens. If both maintain course, they die in a crash. But if one player swerves while the other maintains course, the swerving player is a chicken and the other is a proud winner. The strategy is that each player will claim that she will never swerve and is even willing to die as a means to get the other player to swerve. The structure of the game induces players into this dangerous behavior.

And so it is with the phone game. When the phone rings, each worker wants to convince the others that he will not answer it. The office looks bad if no one answers, so each player wants to hold out and see who is more chicken. And inevitably some calls will be lost during this game.

How To Solve The Phones?

The phone system created a game of chicken with free riders. The structure of the game made it natural for people to avoid answering phones. Will yelling at the employees make a difference? Probably not! The game structure will be the same: people respond more to incentives than to yelling.

The administrator could change the game by assigning individual responsibility. For instance, a schedule could be made where each person covered the phone for one or two hours a day. If someone has to attend a meeting, make it his responsibility to find a person to cover. This new game eliminates both the free rider problem and the game of chicken, and I bet few, if any, calls would be missed.

Before you start yelling at someone for their behavior, see why they are acting that way. Change the game and everyone can win.

4 Tips For Winning A Game Of Chicken

In the last example, the situation of who would answer the office phone became a game of chicken. No one wanted to volunteer, and that resulted in several dropped calls. In a game of chicken, people try to prove they are tougher than other players, and that is a recipe for disaster if no one relents. So in general, it is best to avoid playing games of chicken or change the game into something else.

But unfortunately games of chicken cannot always be avoided. There are games of chicken in schoolyard fights, drinking contests, and negative campaigns, to name a few. In a competitive world, one will be faced with games of chicken and it is best to know strategies to play effectively.

1. Make Yourself Immovable

In the game of chicken, flexibility is a weakness. One of the best solutions is to prove that you will not change course. There is a great story about a standoff between a US and Canadian (CND) ship.

> US Ship: Please change course 0.5 degrees to the south to avoid a collision.

> CND reply: Recommend you divert your course 15 degrees to the South to avoid a collision.

> US Ship: This is the Captain of a US Navy Ship. I say again, divert your course.

> CND reply: No. I say again, you divert YOUR course!

> US Ship: THIS IS THE AIRCRAFT CARRIER USS CORAL SEA, WE ARE A LARGE WARSHIP OF THE US NAVY. DIVERT YOUR COURSE NOW!!

> CND reply: This is a lighthouse. Your call.

While the story is amusing, it turns out to be an urban legend. Nevertheless, the situation demonstrates a strategic lesson: limiting your options, and metaphorically becoming immovable like a lighthouse, can show the other side that you will not back down.

In the game of chicken where two cars head toward each other, one of the drivers could become immovable by advertising he is using a steering wheel lock or even by detaching the wheel and throwing it away. If you saw the other driver could not possible change course, wouldn't you be sure to swerve out of the way?

2. Get A Reputation For Being Tough

Consider a consumer that comes up with a frivolous lawsuit against a big company with damages on the order of $100,000. Should he pursue action? The lawsuit will put both the consumer and the company in a game of chicken. The loser is the side that backs out, but if neither backs out, the consumer may end up wasting time and legal fees and the company may lose out from negative publicity. Of course, the company can decide the whole process is too risky and simply settle out of court.

The result of that course, unfortunately, would be consumers raising more frivolous lawsuits in the hopes of out of court settlement. One of the ways a company can get out of this cycle and win is by creating a reputation for being "tough" by pursuing all lawsuits. The strategy may come at the cost of some losses and some bad publicity, but the long-term effect of fewer lawsuits may be a net gain.

3. Go For Broke

In the movie *Nothing to Lose*, a robber played by Martin Lawrence is trying to steal the car of Tim Robbin's character at gunpoint. The situation is a game of chicken: the person that relents will not get the car, but if neither relents the gun may go off and there may be bloodshed— Robbin's character would die and Lawrence's character would have to face murder charges.

Robbin's character wins the game by announcing that he will not give up. He explains he has just learned very bad news and he therefore has nothing to lose. Then, in a strange twist to prove his point, he kidnaps the robber and takes him to the desert. The fate of the mismatched couple is joined and movie hilarity ensues.

The player that has nothing to lose is more dangerous and such threats will be taken more seriously.

4. Raise The Risk To Your Actions (Brinkmanship)

Brinkmanship is a strategic move where you raise the risk of the game—bringing everyone closer to the brink—unless the other side relents. While you may prefer not to use these "scare tactics," you should understand them because your opponents may employ them.

An interesting example of brinkmanship took place in New Jersey in 2009. The electric supplier PSE&G was proposing a large expansion to a transmission line and seeking a rate increase (the Susquehanna-Roseland transmission line). Taxpayers were not sure about the project. The situation was similar to a game of chicken: the side that relents would lose out on money, but if both sides continued a protracted regulatory battle, then they both would lose by delaying other constructive means for improving the system.

PSE&G made their demands vivid in an advertisement displaying brinkmanship. On January 15, 2009, PSE&G ran an ad in the *Star-Ledger* indicating that if the transmission project did not pass, then residents might face outages like the 2000 blackouts in California or the 2003 blackout in the Northeast. The idea of the ad was to make a threat by raising risk. It would be unpopular (and illegal) for an electric company to create blackouts because it did not get its project passed. The ad sent the message that without action, PSE&G would not have enough control, and therefore everyone would get closer to the brink—electric companies and taxpayers alike. The ad was one part of the campaign for regulatory and public approval. As of November 2013, construction for the transmission line was in progress.

Sources

"The Lighthouse Joke." America's Navy Website, 2 Sept. 2009. Web.
http://www.navy.mil/navydata/nav_legacy.asp?id=174

"PSE&G Proposed Transmission Line Upgrade, & Their Scare Tactics." New Jersey On-Line, LLC. New Jersey Voices Public Blog, 17 Jan. 2007. Web.
http://blog.nj.com/njv_publicblog/2009/01/psegs_proposed_transmission_li.html

Credible Threats

To win a game of chicken, the strategy is to appear tough, and very importantly, get the other person to believe that. The ability to get other people to believe you is useful in many situations, and this is a natural transition into the game theory concept of credibility.

Threats can fall into two categories: credible and non-credible. A threat is *credible* if it will likely be followed through. For instance, when a utility company threatens to disconnect your service for non-payment, it is credible since it can and often does follow through.

A threat is *non-credible* if the opposite holds: you cannot believe it since it is unlikely it will be followed through. These threats are made to encourage behavior, but a savvy person would not believe them. For instance, a defense attorney may threaten that her client will drag a matter out in court—no matter what the evidence is—to encourage the prosecution to consider out of court settlements. But the threat is not credible because if strong evidence comes out, the defense will most likely bargain.

There are two main results: (1) you should only consider credible threats in your decision-making, and (2) threats are credible only if you would follow through on them.

On a practical matter, you can achieve your goals by making your threats appear credible, even if they are non-credible. Here are five methods to make your threats more believable.

Method 1: Have An Alternative

Nothing scares a seller like when you threaten to run a competitor. If you want to negotiate a lower cable rate, internet connection, or better deal on a car, tell the seller your other offer, convince them you really want to stay but are willing to switch (even if you are not), and see how often they cave in.

I'm sure most of you have been in this position and succeeded at some point so I will not belabor it. The truth is, if you have a true alternative, you do not need game theory to help you. I will continue with methods that give you the illusion of leverage even when you do not have it.

Method 2: Use A "Risky Threat"

One summer I was a counselor of a month-long camp for high-school students at Stanford University. Being in charge of thirty high-school students is not easy because we counselors had few real punishments we could dispense.

For mild misbehavior, we would often threaten to call an unruly camper's parents. Most campers fell in line because they were scared. But in reality, this was a non-credible threat. A call to parents would not only anger the parents, who were spending good money for this camp, but it would raise questions to our boss, who might wonder if we were bad counselors.

There were of course some kids who still misbehaved repeatedly— perhaps they figured out our hollow threat. We devised a better solution for them: we threatened that we'd tell college admissions officers about their poor character, which would ruin their chances of getting in. Now, I did not know if college officers kept such admission files, but neither did they, and it would have been really hard for them to find out. In that uncertainty, the threat was very effective: I've never seen students turn obedient so fast.

Method 3: Suggest You Have Alternatives

One of my friends received a job offer during college. It was from his top company choice. The only problem was the offer did not contain a signing bonus. My friend had heard the company did, in fact, give signing bonuses to some new employees.

My friend was in a bind. He did not want to negotiate the offer directly because he might tip his genuine interest, which would make the company unlikely to improve the offer. He was at a slight advantage because, through interviews and congratulations calls, he was sure the company had a large interest in him.

My friend had two weeks to decide on the offer. He contacted the company and indicated the offer was nice, but he needed more time to think about it. He asked for a small extension and indirectly suggested he was considering other offers.

The company soon offered him a signing bonus and called him to encourage he work for them. And he did.

I will offer caution with this method: there are companies that direct negotiation might work better since it is a more straight-forward method, and some companies are so powerful that they will not cave in. My friend suspected he was better off hiding his true interest and that his company would give him the standard signing bonus.

Method 4: Threaten To Go Public

Someone I know had a terrible experience with a cell phone company. The phone they sent him was defective, and when he sent the phone back to them, they denied responsibility and claimed there was water damage on the phone (which there wasn't).

The evidence, of course, was in the company possession, so it was hard for my friend to disprove. After days of failing to get a reasonable response, my friend decided to raise the stakes. He got in touch with a large newspaper and found a reporter willing to write about the story.

My friend contacted a high ranking executive at the cell phone company, told his situation, and suggested that his newspaper contact would pick up the story if he did not get a favorable resolution. He quickly received a written apology from the executive and more than enough compensation for his trouble.

Method 5: Appear Crazy (At Your Own Risk)

The normal economic assumption is that people maximize utility or profits. Given a choice of ten cents or no cents, a person would choose ten cents, regardless of what opponents get.

Consider the following game, known as the ultimatum game. We will explain this game a bit more in the next section. For now, we cover the basic idea. In the game, there is $1 at stake, and your opponent offers you a take-it or leave-it portion of the dollar. If you accept the split, then you keep your portion, and your opponent gets the rest. If you reject, the $1 is burned and both of you go home with nothing.

The game theory solution is that your opponent offers you one cent (or no cents) and you accept. You do not care that you are taken advantage of because, rationally, taking home some money is better than rejecting and taking home nothing. So even if you think a one cent offer is unfair, you do not exact vengeance by rejecting.

But let's say you threaten that if you do not get at least 50 cents you will definitely reject the offer. The threat is non-credible if you are rational and profit-maximizing. But if you are insane, it may be credible. So getting perceived as irrational may give you a more convincing threat and a larger payoff.

Thomas Schelling (of the "focal/Schelling points" fame) came up with the idea that appearing insane might be a strategic advantage. This thinking is powerful, and it may have influenced Nixon in the Madman theory of foreign policy.

I say to use this method with extreme caution because being labeled irrational may hurt your brand in unintended ways. You may win a small battle since you are insane, but then coworkers may never want to work with you.

In other words, sometimes it is better to lose the game at hand to preserve your reputation for the long view.

The Ultimatum Game

Once during college, an annoying person asked me for game theory help. I offered to help even though it interrupted my own work. It was hard to turn down someone who lived in the same dorm.

I offered to help but wanted something in exchange. The person was a teaching assistant for a non-credit class my friends were taking. He was not being fair to my friends and essentially using his power to fulfill a personal grudge. I asked that he be nicer to my friends and act more professionally. He was furious at my suggestion since he felt it undermined his authority.

So I said I would not help him. I reminded him that I had work to do, so if he could not compensate me for my time, I would resume my studies.

He angrily responded that he did not need my help after all. He actually knew how to do the problem, he indicated, but he just wanted my perspective. And, he continued, the professor was holding office hours the next day, so he would ask someone smarter.

He then walked away, sort of.

As I resumed my studies, he conspicuously sat down at a neighboring table and faked that he was doing work. Every few minutes he peeked over his book to see if I would budge.

But I did not.

After thirty minutes, someone who saw the whole thing came up to me and said, "Presh, I can't believe you aren't helping him with game theory. I mean, I know you don't like him, but come on. He needs your help."

To which I replied, "I *am* helping him. If he knew anything about game theory, he would know that I'm not going to tutor him unless he concedes to my request."

On hearing this, the annoying person left the room and never asked me for help again.

I guess he did not really need my help after all.

I chose my actions because I had total negotiating power—a concept from *the ultimatum game*.

I Am The Decider!

Imagine you are participating in a college experiment. The researcher hands you $10. You are instructed to propose a split of the money to another person. For instance, you might propose that you keep $7 and the other person gets $3.

If the other person accepts the division, the money is split according to the proposal. If the other person rejects the division, neither person gets anything.

How might you go about deciding a split?

The first thing you can do is diagram the game dynamics.

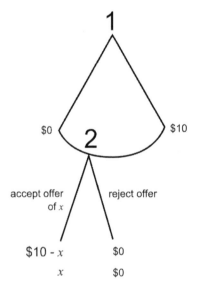

You are player 1 and will offer money to player 2, an amount between $0.01 and $10. After hearing the offer, player 2 can either accept so the split goes through, or reject and leave both parties with nothing.

The way to read the diagram is from top to bottom: the player depicted in the topmost move goes first, and then the next player goes. However, to solve the game, you want to read the diagram in exactly the opposite way: from bottom to top. Since you start at the end, this technique for solving a game is called *backwards induction*.

What offers will player 2 accept?

If he rejects an offer, he goes home with nothing. If he cares about getting money, this would suggest that player 2's strategy is to accept any offer that player 1 makes. Even if the offer is for one cent, that is better monetarily than going home with nothing.

In the land of infinite rationality, player 1 understands this, and takes advantage of his bargaining power. Knowing any offer will be accepted, player 1 will offer the smallest amount to player 2—one cent—and basically take the entire pot for himself.

This solution—player 1 gets everything and player 2 gets nothing—is why the game is called the "ultimatum game." Player 1 has complete negotiating power and knows any ultimatum will be accepted.

But Doesn't Player 2 Have The Power To Punish?

The situation stinks for player 2. It just does not seem fair that player 1 gets everything. I mean, player 2 does have the ability to punish player 1 by rejecting offers. Can that lessen player 1's power?

Imagine player 2 tries to gain power. Before the game starts, player 2 might try to taunt to player 1, "Hey, if you offer me less than a 50-50 split, I will reject it. I don't care if I go home with nothing; I'll just be happy to know that I hurt you."

In the theoretical world, player 1 understands this is a non-credible threat. If player 1 does offer a smaller amount, then player 2 faces a one-time decision of some money or no money. In this world, it only matters that one cent is better than nothing. There is no joy in inflicting pain on the other player. And because the game is not repeated, there is no reason player 2 should even care about punishing player 1.

As a technical aside, each offer that player 1 makes actually is a "subgame" where player 2 has to make a decision. Since player 1 always offers one cent and player 2 always accepts, we never observe what would happen if player 1 offers two cents or more.

In theory, player 2 could do whatever he wants—he could reject those higher offers. But as argued above, the only credible thing player 2 would do in any subgame is to accept the offer.

So we call the equilibrium where player 2 accepts any offer and player 1 gets everything the *subgame perfect equilibrium*. In this game, it is the unique subgame perfect equilibrium.

But That Is Simply Not What Happens In Real Life!

Yes, imagine you are playing this game with your crazy significant other, who is the role of player 2. From experience, you know that your significant other might even reject offers where you give less than 90% of the money.

You'd be wise to forget the subgame perfect equilibrium stuff and make sure to adjust your offer. Your significant other is crazy, after all.

Indeed, experimenters have repeatedly shown that the subgame perfect equilibrium does not happen because people reject offers perceived to be unfair.

But I believe these experiments do not mean game theory is wrong. In fact, they illustrate why game theory is a powerful tool.

It Is All About the Beliefs

A Nash equilibrium is based on your *beliefs* about other players, and how accurate those beliefs are. The subgame perfect equilibrium is the only Nash equilibrium where both players have infinite reasoning ability and they only care about money.

What people seem to miss is that the ultimatum game really has an infinite number of Nash equilibria.

Let's go back to the game with you and your crazy significant other. Your strategies are something like the following.

Significant Other: "Give me at least 90%, or I reject."

You: "I will make sure my offer is not rejected. I surely want to leave with some money."

If you really believe the threat, and it is accurate, the resulting division is a Nash equilibrium of the game. Your significant other is not playing rationally, but the result of you getting $1 and your significant other getting $9 is in fact a Nash equilibrium.

The threat to reject *should* be non-credible, except that your significant other cares more about money, including things like power and fairness. There is power in being perceived as crazy.

When Does This Game Happen In Real Life?

The game happens all the time in homes. My brother and I would be arguing about something, like what video game to play. Eventually, my parents would tell us that we could either agree on a game or we would not get to play at all. My older brother would often speak first and pick a game that only he would like. And I was stuck with the game because it was still better than nothing.

A similar situation happens with labor strikes. The boss offers terms to workers. If the workers accept, then both workers and the company profit. If the workers reject and go on strike, both sides get nothing and lose money while waiting.

An example of this is the 2007-2008 strike of the writers in Hollywood (called the Writer's Guild of America strike). While the writers went on strike, both the writers and studios lost a lot of money. For instance, the canceled Golden Globes that year was estimated to be a $75-million to $100-million loss to the L.A. economy.

And just like in the ultimatum game, while the strike persisted, each side tried to gather negotiating power by tricking the other side about what it truly believes. Each side wanted to demonstrate to the other that it would reject solutions that were deemed unfair, even if that action appeared crazy.

As stated on the blog of James D. Miller, the producers were showing they were committed to a prolonged strike. One of their weapons was siding with Rupert Murdoch, a business magnate who is perceived as a hard line negotiator.

In response, the writers were drumming up their beliefs to high ideals such as a war on labor using a socialist argument. It was unlikely the writers were actually devoted to socialism, as they mostly are fine working within the rules of a capitalist economy. The socialist claims may have helped them appear intransigent, which would have helped their negotiating power.

Who ended up winning? According to a piece in *The New York Times*, it appears that both sides played a pretty hard line and each had to compromise. Writers ended up winning a higher percentage of digital sales for the long run, but they lost out on money in the short-run for traditional distribution. The ultimatum game can definitely get ugly sometimes.

Sources

Experimental result of ultimatum game: Oosterbeek, Hessel, Randolph Sloof, and Gijs Van De Kuilen. "Cultural differences in ultimatum game experiments: Evidence from a meta-analysis." *Experimental Economics* 7.2 (2004): 171-188.

Carr, David. "Who Won the Writers Strike?" *New York Times*. 12 Feb 2008. Web. http://www.nytimes.com/2008/02/12/arts/television/12strike.html

The Writer's Strike and Game Theory. James D. Miller. 04 Jan 2008. Web. http://jamesdmiller.blogspot.com/2008/01/writers-strike-and-game-theory.html

Gossip Wars And Mutually Assured Destruction (MAD)

There is one method of making a threat credible that deserves special treatment. The topic is mutually assured destruction (MAD) and will be described extensively in the context of nuclear deterrence and gossip wars.

Growing up, I wanted to be like Michael Jordan. I think that was the dream of every kid I knew. We wanted the shoes. We drank the Gatorade (literally) and ate McDonald's. We stuck our tongues out on the court.

Okay, so none of that really worked. But we weren't wrong about wanting to be like Jordan. We merely focused on the wrong details. We should have been learning to copy his media relations off-court.

One could argue that Jordan's genius was as much about public relations as it was about basketball. He handled bad publicity and gossip wars better than anybody.

What was one of Air Jordan's secrets? It is not something most athletes nowadays do: it was being silent and avoiding gossip wars.

When the media reported a bad story, he would generally back off and say nothing. This advice is easy to state, but it is extremely hard to follow. Most people get defensive from simple criticism. Think about the restraint necessary to shut up about affairs sorted out in the public media. And that is essentially what Jordan was able to do.

I will give more details about Jordan at the end of the article. I first want to take a step back and consider why the strategy works. I liken the scenario to a game theory concept of deterrence in military games. I break the discussion into two areas.

The first is mutually assured destruction (MAD). This is one doctrine for deterrence in a nuclear world.

The second is gossip wars. These are more routine situations that start with escalations and end up in games of MAD.

Mutually Assured Destruction (MAD)

MAD is a way to achieve peace on facing the threat of nuclear annihilation. It is often used to describe the peace between America and the Soviet Union during the Cold War.

The game is as follows: America and the Soviet Union are engaging in a nuclear arms race. At any moment, both countries are choosing whether to maintain peace ("back off") or to launch missiles ("strike").

If both countries "back off," then the status quo is maintained and nothing happens. That's the only peaceful outcome.

If either country is defiant enough to "strike," then both countries will engage in all-out nuclear warfare until mutual death. The theory is that a unilateral strike will ruin any future hope of reconciliation. Because any strike will lead to mutual death, the game earns the name "mutually assured destruction."

The game can be represented as a game tree. Here is the diagram.

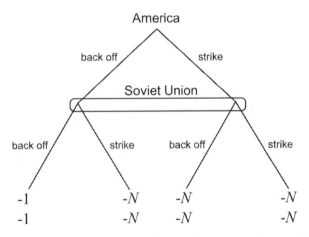

Let me explain this diagram. The diagram is meant to be read from top to bottom. The United States can either choose to "back off" or to "strike." The other player is Soviet Union, and the Soviet Union chooses "back off" or "strike" as well. Once both make their choices, the game has payouts to each player.

The payoff of $-N$ denotes a very destructive outcome to both sides (you can think about it like negative one million). The payoff of -1 indicates peace but with tension. The number choices are arbitrary—the idea is that peace is good and nuclear strikes are very bad.

The game tree has one noteworthy feature: the nodes for the Soviet Union's choices are circled. This is to indicate the simultaneous aspect of the game—the Soviet Union chooses at the same time America does.

If the circle was not drawn, the interpretation would be that of a sequential game. That is, the Soviet Union would be making a choice *after observing* America's choice.

For this particular game, it is important to model the action as simultaneous. Sequential games often have different outcomes.

Nash Equilibria

How will this game play out? As usual, we think about how each player would best respond to the opposing player's actions.

If the other country chooses "back off," then the choice is between "back off," which leads to peace, and "strike" which leads to world destruction. The logical choice is "back off."

What if the other country picks "strike"? In this case, the world would be destroyed regardless. Either choice of "back off" or "strike" is reasonable.

In summary,

--The strategy "back off" is a best response to "back off."

--The strategies "back off" or "strike" are best responses to "strike."

An equilibrium occurs when both countries are picking best responses. Two cases jump out as equilibria: when both pick "back off" for peace or when both pick "strike" and get mutual death.

There is only one more case to consider: one country picks "back off" and the other picks "strike." Could this be an equilibrium? The answer is no. The best response to "back off" is "back off;" hence, the country picking "strike" is not choosing a best response.

Thus, the two equilibria of the game are both picking "back off" or both picking "strike." In the following figure this is illustrated by the solid lines. The dashed lines are paths off the equilibrium path.

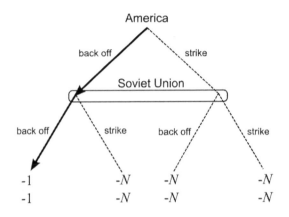

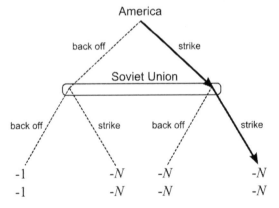

Interpretation

There are two Nash equilibria to the game: one ensuring peace and one leading to world destruction. To sane people, the peace option is clearly preferred.

You might think the world destruction is just a footnote as no one would want it to happen. But that is not true. The world destruction equilibrium is actually *crucial* to obtaining peace. Well, that is the principle of MAD, anyway.

It has to do with credible threats. For example, most kids know a parental threat of being kicked out of the house is not going to happen—it is non-credible. The parent's best response to misbehavior is discipline, not kicking them out of the house. Hence, the threat fails to change behavior.

In contrast, in MAD, nuclear retaliation *is* credible because it *is* a best response. It is because annihilation is an equilibrium that both countries fear retaliation and choose peace.

MAD is a controversial principle. I'll briefly touch on two issues.

First, it is an unsettling situation. A small miscommunication could trigger mistrust and quickly turn into world destruction. That is a high stakes game.

Second, both countries are expending lots of money to build up arms in the first place. If peace is the desired outcome, then both countries are spending money simply to stockpile. That does not seem the most efficient way to get peace.

But do not get too caught up in the details of MAD as a nuclear war game. As I will discuss next, MAD comes up in life games too, such as "gossip wars."

MAD In Gossip Wars

We do not play high-stakes games in our daily routine. More realistically, we face small escalations and retaliations until a boiling point is reached. That stage is essentially a game of MAD.

One such example is a "gossip war" between two people, such as two best friends, a child and a parent, a husband and a wife, or the media and a celebrity. I will use the last example as the framework, but the analysis can apply to any of those situations.

Here is how a gossip war works. In "peacetime," the celebrity and the media work together. Profitable, peaceful stories keep both sides happy and exclusive access and publicity are traded freely.

But occasionally, the celebrity is implicated in controversial rumors.

They could be true or not—what's important is that spreading the news would hurt the celebrity's image and give the media marginally higher profits.

To start the game, the media has a choice. One choice is to simply "back off" the story and keep the peace. The other choice is to report the rumor and hence "escalate" the relationship with the celebrity.

If the story is reported, the celebrity also has two choices to respond. Once choice is to "back off" and take a small reputation hit. The other option is to publicly deny the claim and "escalate" the matter again.

If both the media and celebrity choose to escalate the matter, the situation will turn into a full-blown media extravaganza. There will be name-calling, wild allegations, and juicy stories that are completely unrelated. In short, it will be a "gossip war."

The gossip war is analogous to a nuclear war. If both sides "back off," the matter will be settled in peace at a small cost. If, however, either side "strikes" with damaging evidence—then both reputations will be substantially damaged. The celebrity will get washed up, and the media will lose out on future stories about the celebrity.

How does this game play out? Here is the game presented as a tree.

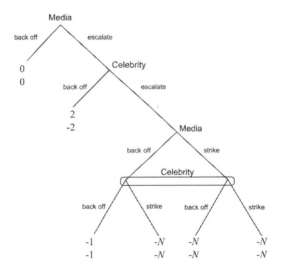

Like the MAD game above, the payoff choices are somewhat arbitrary. But here is the overarching logic for the payoffs.

--An initial media back off means no change so each party gets zero.

--A media escalation followed by celebrity back off gives the media some profit (2) at the expense of the celebrity (-2).

--The peace outcome of the gossip war is better for the celebrity (-1) than backing off just prior (-2). And conversely, the peace outcome for the media (-1) is worse than if the celebrity had not backed off (2).

Nash Equilibrium

We can analyze the game by using backwards induction. This essentially means beginning from the bottom of the tree and proceeding upward.

The last phase, if reached, is a gossip war. The equilibria are analogous to the MAD game: with either both players choosing "back off" or both choosing "strike." The two cases should be analyzed separately.

First case: The "back off" equilibrium will be reached.

Moving up the tree, what would the celebrity do if the media escalates? Knowing the gossip war will end in peace, the celebrity would prefer the choice to escalate (ends up as -1) rather than to backing off (ends up as -2). Going up one step, the media would anticipate the celebrity's retaliation, and at the start of the game, decide backing off the rumor (payoff 0) is better than escalating (payoff -1).

Here is the reasoning illustrated, with the optimal branches highlighted.

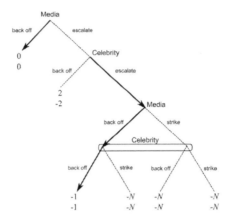

Second case: The "strike" equilibrium will be reached.

Moving up the tree, what would the celebrity do if the media escalates? Knowing the gossip war will end in destruction, the celebrity would rather back off (ends up as -2) than escalate (ends up as negative infinity). Going up one step, the media would anticipate the celebrity's backing off, and realize it is better to escalate (payoff 2) than back off (payoff 0).

Here is the reasoning illustrated, with the optimal branches highlighted.

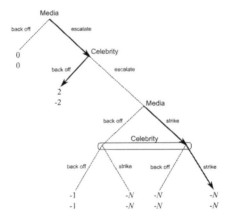

Interpretation

Which equilibrium path is likely to be reached? Well, it depends on the celebrity and the media. I imagine that most celebrities and media members are vindictive and would escalate the gossip war into mutual destruction. Using this logic, that means the second case is more likely.

This means the media is likely to escalate all news and in response celebrities will be best served by shutting up about allegations. Even if that means taking a small reputation hit, it is better to minimize losses than face a destructive gossip war. Of course, most celebrities tend to escalate the matter by calling news conferences and creating a publicity storm.

Conclusion

We all know the great basketball side of Jordan. But on the sidelines, he was shrewdly playing the gossip war game and backing off each time. According to an article from the sports writer Skip Bayless, Michael Jordan avoided gossip wars with the media by refusing to respond to any questions. In this manner, both Jordan and the media profited from Jordan's image.

I can honestly say I have used this analysis to better my life. I find myself responding to escalations all the time, and mostly, I am disciplined enough to back away. Before I understood the high-stakes nature of the game, this wasn't always the case. I have burned bridges and lost friends out of gossip wars—more than I would like to admit. To think, I could have salvaged those situations just by staying quiet.

Here is my appeal: if you feel slighted by a small rumor from a friend, family member, or the media, see if you can back off and take the loss. If possible, do not feed the flame and avoid the gossip war.

No matter how slighted I feel, I think of Jordan and minimize my losses. The chance of a single blow-up is not worth it.

Source

Bayless, Skip. "Jordan Rules Compared to Kobe." ESPN.com. Page 2. 17 Dec. 2004. Web. http://sports.espn.go.com/espn/page2/story?page=bayless/041217

Honesty Isn't The Best Policy

Whoever said "honesty is the best policy" had to be lying, and never learned the game theory of credible threats. Lies have saved many messengers from being shot, and many couples from explosive arguments about body image.

There is certainly much to be said about honesty as a moral principle. I encourage you to be as honest as you are comfortable with.

The problem is that we do not live in theory—we need to asses matters practically. And in this light, game theory suggests that lies can be beneficial to all parties. In many cases, a policy of occasionally lying is more effective than a policy of strict honesty.

The reason is that lies can paradoxically make the threats more credible. I want to discuss two examples of effective lies.

Effective Lie #1: "Give me a lower rate or I'm canceling!"

There are some picky customers that seek perfection, the so-called "rate-chasers." Most of us are content to pay a reasonable price for good service, and that means paying a little extra to avoid the hassle of switching to an imperfect competitor.

Most customers are lying when they claim they will cancel. The truth is they want a lower rate, but how can they make it possible?

A customer could list all the reasons a lower rate is beneficial for both sides. The business avoids customer acquisition costs. The customer does not have to change service.

But these truths are not enough to convince a business. And so the honest reasons need to be emphasized by the dishonest threat of leaving.

I have made several calls where I have threatened to cancel and the agent knew it was a hollow threat. Nonetheless, the lie was a good enough threat and I was able to get a good discount.

Effective Lie #2: "I'll never be with you—ever!"

My friend in college was crushed. Things were going so well with the woman he was interested in. But things fell apart when he wanted to make it more serious. She was stunned at the situation and really not interested in him.

They had "the talk" where she indicated her interest was friendly and not romantic. And she even went further and told him that she would never be with him—ever. It was this last statement that particularly bothered my friend, as it gave him no hope.

He vented his feelings with me and I was thinking about how to make him feel better. How could I get him out of the rut?

First I suggested if they really were a good match, they might work out over time. Second, I wanted him to think strategically. When she said they would never be together, it was probably not the end of the game.

Why was I so sure of the first reason? I told my friend no one can predict the future. There are thousands of stories and movies about women that change feelings about men. People change over time. She could not possibly predict the person she would be in a few years, so how can she claim to never be interested in him?

And that brings the second part: why did she say "never" in the first place? The reason is that the slight fib made the truth more convincing. She had already told my friend she was not interested and needed a stronger signal.

Besides, what was her alternative? If she told him that she could see them together in the future, then she would be sending too optimistic a message. She needed to discuss the future to ensure my friend stopped going after her in the present.

Here is my summary of it all: take heart if you are rejected, but know your best response might be to move on in the short term.

Threatening Many People At Once

In a game of chicken and many situations in life, you only need to prove your threat is credible to one or a few people. This will not do, however, in some games where you face many opponents. There will be more people to threaten and more people who will wish to prove your threat is not credible. How do you win this game?

A concrete example took place in 2007 when the Recording Industry Association of America (RIAA) won a legal battle about music piracy. A Minnesota woman was found guilty of copyright infringement for file sharing and fined for damages of $220,000. Although the award was significantly smaller than the requested $3.9 million plus legal fees, the RIAA considered the case a victory. Was it a victory, and would it deter illegal file sharing?

The problem is interesting from a game theory perspective. The situation is something of a guessing game. The RIAA would like to prosecute every illegal downloader, but then monitoring and legal fees would be exorbitantly high. People would also like to download songs for free, but only if the risk of being caught is low. Without enforcement illegal downloads are high, so the RIAA would choose to monitor more, but that discourages people from downloading, which allows the RIAA to save costs by lowering enforcement, and the cycle continues.

The problem is similar to cops who want to prevent people from speeding. What tends to happen is that cops monitor at a level high enough to discourage rampant speeding but low enough to minimize costs. In this kind of game, high enforcement costs mean we have to live with some people speeding. But suppose the RIAA is not happy with the "optimal" level of illegal downloads and wants to stamp out even more people. What kind of strategy might it pursue?

For starters, the RIAA needs to threaten many people at the same time and one way to do this is what I call the "principle of embarrassment." I first learned about it from a motivation speaker during high school. At the start of an assembly, our speaker politely asked us to be quiet to no avail. We kept chatting because we felt safety in numbers: each of us felt immunity as one of 1,000 audience members. Then the speaker then did something that made everyone dead silent.

In a strong and somewhat angry voice, he pointed to a popular student and called him on stage. The speaker made fun of him for talking until we were all laughing. I can still remember the student's look of embarrassment. It was effective enough that the rest of us dared not say a word for fear we would be the next one on stage.

By embarrassing one student, the speaker was able to threaten all of us. In theory, this strategy could work for the RIAA, and this appears to be what the RIAA was doing by prosecuting individuals very publicly. But if that was the case, the RIAA may have misapplied the theory as its situation was lacking three vital elements that make the "principle of embarrassment" work.

The principle of embarrassment can be described as a strategic move that turns a simultaneous game (trying to silence every student at once) into a sequential game (silencing one student and telling every other student they could be "next in line"). Here are some tips when using this strategic move.

1. The Penalty Should Be Enforced Quickly

During the assembly, the speaker immediately punished the popular student to get his message across. The RIAA lacked the advantage of speed. The legal victory in 2007 was the result of a case that started two years before in 2005.

What the RIAA did is analogous to the speaker taking the student aside, going through two years of school board meetings, and then giving him a detention when most of us were already in college. This result would neither have deterred us from chatting during the presentation nor would it serve as much of a lesson to incoming students.

2. The Target Audience Should Witness The Punishment

The speaker was able to send a message to us in the audience since we were watching him humiliate our peer.

The RIAA, on the other hand, went after a thirty year old single parent and that does not necessarily send the message to the majority of people who download songs illegally, like college students.

3. The Threat To Repeat Punishment Has To Be Credible

This is a very important step. During the assembly, we were scared since the speaker had no hesitation to bring students on stage. It was easy and costless for him to do, and he seemed to enjoy making fun of us high school students.

Was the RIAA threat credible? The RIAA faces legal fees and court time for each offender it prosecutes. It is not reasonable the RIAA would actually go after each and every offender.

One Last Note

Even if the RIAA did apply the principle of embarrassment correctly, it might still have taken a hit from having a reputation of "bullying" individuals. The woman in the current case was fined $220,000 for sharing 24 songs and was widely perceived as an excessive fine. It is not easy to threaten many people at once.

The Strategy Of Limiting Options

The idea of making your threat credible is that you want to prove you will not back down. One way this can be achieved is by *intentionally limiting your options* to improve your bargaining position.

A short story will illustrate the strategy. Consider the following situation: John and Tim are both finishing projects at a consulting company and they are ready to be staffed on new projects. Their skill-sets and work ethics are similar, and both are considered team-players. Though they are comparable employees, their projects have been very different. For the last year, Tim has been stuck on projects with repetitious tasks, like gathering data, while John has been able to enjoy exciting projects with travel to places like Hawaii.

Tim's poor fate is all too common. I suspect you too have a similar experience where a fellow coworker of similar talent gets better work than you.

I wonder why some people get cooler projects. Often, it is the case that good projects simply go to talented employees and likeable employees. I bet this obvious explanation explains much of staffing choices. But it is only part of the story.

How does a company staff employees of similar talent, like John and Tim? Luck may play a role, but I doubt companies are tossing coins and randomly staffing projects. Ultimately, managers and coordinators decide staffing and they make decisions based on how the people they staff will react. Is there a way John could influence their decision to staff him on better projects?

The answer has to do with why some airline passengers pretend to have special dietary needs, and why Stanford Economics professors were willing to give up authority in teaching their courses.

Airline Food

Airline food jokes are a dime a dozen. I'm not sure why airline food is terrible, but it is probably related to two facts. First, airlines save money by giving passengers the cheapest food. And second, the food is served to everyone and as the saying goes: when you try to please everyone, you end up pleasing no one.

What can you do as a passenger to get better food? You can demonstrate that you are not the average customer by requesting a specialty meal, like vegetarian or kosher food, which are often better than the normal fare.

Why is the special-order food better? It is because you signal your tastes belong to a special group and hence the food is not just the plain meal. For instance, vegetarian food will likely have fresh fruit, which may not be appreciated by all passengers. The essence is that you can improve your food situation on an airline by *limiting your options* of what you say you can eat.

Can we really get better results by limiting our options? Let's consider how Stanford Economics professors made themselves happier by limiting their authority.

Stanford University Economics Professors

University professors are a proud bunch. They pride themselves on intellectual and social freedom. One of my professors confessed to me that he did not want corporate work since he could not survive with a direct boss controlling his work. Professors relish freedom, and in fact, it is this freedom that allows tenured professors to take risks, like discussing new perspectives on controversial political issues.

Naturally, you might think that professors would want freedom to teach their classes however they see fit. So why did Stanford Economic professors willingly agree to a three-page document dictating course policies like exam attendance and correcting errors in grading?

The truth is that professors do not like dealing with issues like students missing exams and correcting errors in grading. Prior to the rules, they had to think of fair ways to handle many special requests, which they did not even want to consider. By agreeing to the three page set of rules that limits their authority over these issues, the professors could tell students they have no control in the matters. Surprisingly, freedom-loving professors are made better off by *giving up control* and restricting their freedom.

Getting Good Projects

We now return to your employer. If you want to get on better projects, figure out a way to limit your options by becoming *less flexible*. There are many ways to do this.

Perhaps you can subtly voice how unhappy you are in bad projects so you get a reputation of not doing well on them. If you are valued enough on good projects, you will probably be staffed on them over your similarly talented coworker who is less vocal about bad projects.

Alternately, if "bad projects" are those with longer hours, you can try to avoid them by filling your personal schedule with appointments you cannot miss. You limit your flexibility and reduce their chances of staffing you longer hours. You walk a fine line and you have to be careful that people understand the appointments are truly out of your control—like a the exam date for a professional course, or a concert you are playing for—instead of things you could do other times—like a weekend vacation or a non-emergency doctor's appointment.

Limiting Options In Salary Negotiation

My underpaid friend used every trick during salary negotiations to no avail. One year she finally got the raise she deserved. The trick that finally worked was getting sick.

My friend joked the company would only realize her value after she left. By chance, it happened much sooner. My friend became very ill for one week and her projects suffered. Upon her return, she quickly fixed the problems. It was this incident that impressed managers at review time.

The peculiar part of the story is my friend did not really change herself. She did not take a class, or learn a new skill, or even demonstrate a hidden talent—she had cleaned up messes at the office before. What she did inadvertently do by being absent was illustrate her co-workers' incompetence. Negotiating is not always about what you can do but rather what others cannot do.

One of the few credible ways to demonstrate what others cannot do is by withholding supply. This means strategically working less or producing less if you are truly in a position of power. Contrary to popular opinion, working longer and harder is not always the best negotiating tactic.

Withholding supply is a powerful negotiating strategy. It has been used by big players such as Microsoft, Nintendo, the Oakland Athletics, and the clothing retailer Zara. But before we get into these examples, let's explore the theory through a simple card game.

The Card Game

The game is described in the book *Co-Opetition* and is quite interesting. The setup is that 26 MBA students are each handed one red card. The professor, Adam Brandenburger, keeps 26 black cards. The dean is offering a prize of $100 to anyone—either Adam or a student—who can return a red-black pair of cards.

That's the game. It is a free-form negotiation between Adam and the students, as both groups try to acquire the matching card to make a pair. The only stipulation in the game is that the students cannot get together and bargain as a group with Adam. They have to bargain on an individual basis. Where would you expect the negotiations to end up?

At the outset, it would appear Adam has a tremendous advantage. He has all the black cards so all pairs have to be made by trading with him. Adam can therefore exert his power by selling his cards at a premium or buying red cards at a discount. So what price will prevail during the trades?

We can make a guess using game theory. One way to proceed is by calculating how important each player is to the game. The relevant concept is a player's "added value." In this game, the added value is how much money a player's presence contributes to the game. The examples below will make the idea clear.

Let's calculate Adam's added value. Adam has all the black cards. When Adam is in the game, he can contribute to each of the 26 pairs worth a total of $2,600. If Adam were not in the game, then there would be no black cards, and hence no chance for prize money. The difference between the two scenarios is Adam's added value—it is $2,600.

What about each student's added value? Each student has exactly one red card. When that student is in the game, he allows for one pair to be made worth $100 of prize money. If that student were not in the game, then there would be exactly one fewer pair. Therefore, each student's added value is $100. The 26 students combined sum up to an added value of $2,600.

The symmetry in added values of the two sides suggests an even split of power. To make any particular pair, Adam's black card is as important as a student's red card. Adam cannot lowball students because they can hold out until a fair offer is made.

Here is why. Suppose that every pair had been made except the last one. At this stage, both Adam and the student understand there is $100 up for grabs. The student's card is as vital to the prize as Adam's card. Neither side would likely agree to anything less than half of the $100. The result is an even split. Since each student could think this way, every student ends up with half of the prize money for the pair. The prize money is therefore split evenly between Adam and the students.

Can Adam Do Better? Yes-Withhold Supply

Adam's monopoly on black cards surprisingly yields him no more than half of the money. But he can do better, if he withholds supply.

The trick is creating an artificial scarcity of black cards. Imagine Adam burns one of his black cards in front of the students. Now there are only 25 black cards. While burning a card will lower the total prize money by $100, it will provide Adam with incredible negotiating power.

We can see this by calculating the added values. In this setup, Adam still has all the black cards and is necessary in creating each pair of cards. Adam's added value is still the whole pot, which is now $2,500.

What about the students? It is here that things change dramatically. There are 26 red cards but now only 25 black cards. This means one red card is in surplus and will not be paired in the end. If we removed any one student from the game, the total prize money would stay the same. Consequently, each student has an added value of zero. Suddenly, no single student is essential!

Now, the asymmetry in added values of the two sides suggests Adam has much power. No single student's card is essential for making a pair and inevitably one student will be left out at the end. Since any student could end up with nothing, those that end up with any money—even $1—could consider themselves better off.

Another way to see this is by considering the end-game. Suppose 25 of 26 students would have ended up with $50, similar to the outcome of the first scenario. Then there is one student that gets nothing and is left out. It would be in that person's interest to sell the card for less—say $49. When Adam accepts that offer, it will put some other student out of the game. Now that person will sell for even less, say $48, rather than get nothing. In essence, the student that is left out drives down the selling price. Since every student fears getting left out, every student would settle for any money rather than get nothing. And so the price of red cards will drop.

The end result is that Adam can buy the red cards at a steep discount and end up with almost all of $2,500. This is a better individual outcome than getting half of $2,600. The trick was withholding supply to increase negotiating power.

Examples: Microsoft, Nintendo, The Oakland A's, And Zara's

If done right, big companies can similarly withhold supply for individual benefit. The actions are always controversial because withholding supply comes at an expense to society (notice that Adam destroyed $100 of value by burning a card).

It is best to learn from real examples. Here are four ways companies have effectively controlled their supply.

1) Microsoft has long been charged of withholding supply. Randal Picker, at the University of Chicago Law School, describes some tactics of Microsoft and uses the same analogy of the card game about artificial scarcity. One example is that AOL was seeking a deal with Microsoft to promote its online connection services. In theory Microsoft could easily add icons for any internet service provider. But it intentionally limited its icons. Now AOL was competing for a limited spot and Microsoft was able to extract promises that AOL would promote Microsoft's Internet Explorer browser.

2) Nintendo has also been charged with creating artificial scarcity when it introduced the Wii and stores had shortages of it. If Nintendo did withhold supply, what might have been its reason?

Nintendo may have been combating the buying power of big retailers. Stores could not simply order all the Wii units they wanted, but they had to wait for a limited quota. The retailers were turned into students hoping they would not be left out. This would shift the power to Nintendo.

Interestingly, this is not the first time Nintendo has been alleged of withholding supply. Some economists have wondered this about Nintendo since 1997.

3) The Oakland Athletics baseball team is a third example. We can think about selling tickets to a game as a kind of matching game. Each occupied seat is a match between a physical seat and a fan that purchases the ticket. The fans and owners split the value of the seat in some manner. The owners have all the seats (like Adam with the black cards), but it is the fans that have the money to buy the seats. The resulting outcome depends on how desired the seats are. In good times, every game is sold out and ticket prices rise. When demand is poor, people may only buy the cheap seats. It is in this situation that owners can counter by adjusting the number of available seats.

This is what the Oakland Athletics did in 2006 by intentionally blocking out some of the cheaper seats, reducing seating capacity by 22 percent. Average attendance dropped by 10 percent, but that was made up by an increase in average ticket price.

4) Zara's is a Spanish-owned clothing retailer. Typically clothing stores work on the business model of selling in-season clothes at a premium and then clearing inventory at heavy discounts at the season's end. Shoppers have two options: either buy clothes at full price, or wait for the season to end and save when the clothes are on clearance. Zara's did not like this game as it gave shoppers an incentive to wait instead of buying right away. So how did Zara's change the game? It limited the shopper's options, according to an article in *US News & World Report*, by turning over its inventory every three to four weeks. The goal was to train shoppers to buy right away, at full price, by adding a risk the item might not be there the next time. Withhold the supply; hold the power.

Sources

Picker, Randal C., Pursuing a Remedy in Microsoft: The Declining Need for Centralized Coordination in a Networked World (July 2001). A revised version is forthcoming in Journal of Institutional and Theoretical Economics. Available at SSRN: http://ssrn.com/abstract=279179 or http://dx.doi.org/10.2139/ssrn.279179

Ayres, Ian and Nalebuff, Barry J., Common Knowledge As A Barrier To Negotiation (April 1997). Yale ICF Working Paper No. 97-01. Available at SSRN: http://ssrn.com/abstract=36224 or http://dx.doi.org/10.2139/ssrn.36224

Young, Eric. "A's Game Plan – Fewer Fans, More Money—Pays Off." San Francisco Business Times. 10 Sept. 2006. Web. http://www.bizjournals.com/sanfrancisco/stories/2006/09/11/story5.html?page=1&b=1157947200%255E1342603

Palmer, Kimberly. "The Games Companies Play." U.S. News & World Report. 1 Aug. 2007. Web. http://www.usnews.com/usnews/biztech/articles/070801/01companygames.htm

The Braess Paradox

Limiting options can also have unexpectedly good social benefits. During one holiday season, several roads in my town were temporarily closed due to flooding. I was naturally worried how the road closures would affect traffic. But in the end, my fears were unfounded. Not only was traffic mostly unaffected, I often found my travel times were reduced!

This experience made no sense to me. If traffic is about too many cars on the roads, how could blocking some roads speed my commute? Or conversely, why might adding roads slow my commute?

There is an interesting game theoretic explanation of why this might happen, known as the Braess Paradox. It states that it is possible that adding a road could lead to slower travel for all drivers. Let's go through an example to see why.

A Traffic Question

Consider a traffic network where 1,000 drivers wish to travel from *start* to *end*. There are two main paths the drivers can take. They can either travel along the path *start-A-end* or along the path *start-B-end*.

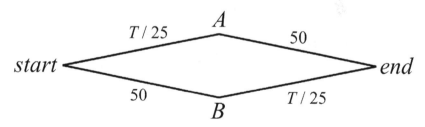

The choice is complicated by the presence of traffic. Some roads are narrow and get congested. On these roads, the travel time for every driver depends on how many travelers T also pick that path. In this network, the roads *start-A* and *B-end* are narrow and travel time is estimated to be $T/25$ minutes on average. The travel on these roads will be slower as more and more drivers choose them.

But not all roads are wide. Some roads are so wide that they never get congested. On these roads, the travel time for every driver will be a constant number of minutes. In this network, the roads *A-end* and *start-B* are wide and travel time is estimated to be 50 minutes on average.

If every driver is optimizing travel times, as is natural in real life, how long will it take to travel from *start* to *end?*

The Nash Equilibrium

The traffic game is dynamic. Each driver has to choose a path by guessing what others will do. We can start the analysis by calculating the travel times of each route dependent on the number of drivers.

If *A* drivers choose the route *start-A-end,* then the route will take *A/25* minutes for *start-A* and then 50 minutes for *A-end.*

Similarly, if *B* drivers choose the route *start-B-end,* then the route will take 50 minutes for *start-B* and then *B/25* minutes for *B-end.*

We can graph the travel times for the two paths as follows.

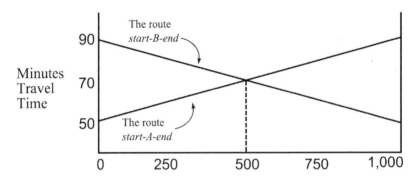

Cars using the route *start-A-end*

In practice, there are many possible outcomes to the traffic game. For instance, it is possible that 600 drivers choose the path *start-A-end* yielding a travel time of 74 minutes. That would mean the other 400 drivers who took *start-B-end* only had a 66 minute drive. But drivers are smart, and with traffic reports they can improve their choice in the future. We can imagine that some of the drivers from the *start-A-end* route would change travel routes the next day.

Such switching will continue as each driver optimizes. The time people stop switching—that is, when the traffic system will be in equilibrium—is therefore when the two driving routes have equal travel times.

We can solve the equations or inspect the graph to see this happens when $A = B = 500$ and both routes have a travel time of **70 minutes**. Now every driver is indifferent between the two choices. Since no driver can improve given what others are doing, this is a Nash equilibrium.

What Happens When You Add A New Road?

Imagine a new road is added between points A and B. We might imagine the road is so wide and small in length that it takes almost no time to traverse it (it is a "free" road).

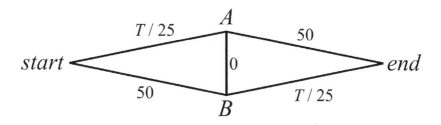

What will happen to the game now?

Solving The New Game (The Braess Paradox)

The new road allows drivers more choice. Now they can switch routes by going along the "free" road. How will the game play out?

The game is surprisingly simple to solve because each driver has a dominant strategy. Consider the first choice of picking the path *start-A* versus *start-B*. We can quickly see that every driver will pick *start-A*. This is because *start-A* takes 40 minutes at worst (if all 1,000 took it, it will take $1,000 / 25 = 40$ minutes) compared to *start-B* which takes 50 minutes for sure. So all drivers pick *start-A* and spend 40 minutes.

What will happen next? Once at A, the drivers have two choices. They can either stick to *A-end* (50 minutes for sure) or they can take the free road *A-B* (0 minutes) and follow the road *B-end* (which takes $T / 25$, and hence will be 40 minutes at worse). Naturally all drivers will choose the free road and *B-end* route.

We can conclude that all 1,000 drivers will take the path *start-A-B-end*. When we calculate the travel times, we find we have a grand total of **80 minutes** ($1,000 / 25 + 0 + 1,000 / 25$).

Additionally, notice that no driver will want to switch because the alternative routes *start-A-end* and *start-B-end* now take 90 minutes each.

In this equilibrium, the roads the travelers pick are completely congested. And consequently this game's equilibrium is 10 minutes worse than before the road *A-B* existed!

What's Going On?

The paradox is the consequence of individual incentives conflicting with the social optimum. If all drivers could agree not to take the "free" road *A-B*, then it would be possible that everyone could save 10 minutes. The problem is this proposal is not sustainable—individual drivers have an incentive to cheat and save time. Eventually the entire system breaks down when everyone cheats, making the roads congested.

The lesson is that social planning is necessary to coordinate drivers for the optimum. And that means it is sometimes best to limit options.

Burning Bridges

There is a saying "never burn bridges," which means never ruin a relationship to the point you can never return. This is largely sensible advice, as it is a small world and you never know when you will bump into that person again. However, the advice is not wholly accurate. In fact, there are many times that burning a bridge is not just beneficial, but absolutely necessary to accomplish a goal. It is an extension of the strategy of limiting options.

In that framework, think about burning bridges as a tool, much like a carpenter views a sledge hammer. Reckless use can causes irreversible damage, but careful use is appropriate and even necessary to begin new construction. Control the tool, as in the following examples, and you can reap the benefits.

Burn Bridges That Never Existed

I saw this strategy enacted many times on *The Daily Show*, a sarcastic comedy news show. The guest was a government official and he was angry with Jon Stewart, the show's host. For weeks, Stewart had been poking fun of the guest for presenting inconsistent facts during news conferences. Armed with an opportunity for revenge, the guest listed a few examples of how *The Daily Show* was inconsistent in its facts. He demanded Stewart provide an explanation for his hypocrisy.

Stewart's answer had to be careful. His answer would influence whether this guest, and others like him, would ever come on the show. If the answer was soft, it might come off as unprofessional. If it was too harsh, it might burn a bridge.

What did Stewart say? Without missing a beat, Stewart mockingly gave the answer: "Here at *The Daily Show*, we... well... we don't check our facts."

The audience immediately burst out into laughter and the guest looked very angry. He had the look of "I can't believe I agreed to this show, and no one I know is going to come on this show again."

Stewart certainly burned a bridge, but this was not bad. The truth is that bridge was one that never existed. *The Daily Show* is not about getting every fact right, but rather about the comedy of politics.

The impact was clear. The guest will likely never return on the show, but the other side is that future guests have never been as confrontational. By committing to his brand, Stewart improved the quality of his future guests.

When Backed Into A Corner, Burn All Bridges Equally

The yardstick for successful people is different than for unsuccessful people. Successful people are criticized for times they fail. Unsuccessful people are praised for times they achieve.

Most actors aspire to be A-listers, the most bankable movie stars. Kathy Griffin, on the other hand, is a self-proclaimed "D-lister." Why such a low standard?

Well, perhaps it is because she has no other choice. Griffin has inadvertently created a reputation for controversy. She has been banned from several talk shows, including the David Letterman show. In addition, she was fired from the E! Entertainment channel in 2005 after making an off-hand remark about Dakota Fanning at an award show.

Backed into a corner, Griffin started burning all kinds of bridges on her show "Kathy Griffin: My Life on the D-List." No one is free from her criticism. According to the *New York Times*, she's made fun of Oprah Winfrey, Conan O'Brien, Ryan Seacrest, Miley Cyrus, Russell Crowe, Hugh Hefner, Nicole Kidman, and even Michael Gelman, executive producer of "Live With Regis and Kelly."

Griffin is using a more extreme version of Stewart's strategy. She has few options remaining, so she can burn more bridges that never existed. And she's apparently doing it effectively. Her show won an Emmy for outstanding noncompetitive reality show.

How You Can Use The Advice

Burning bridges is not just for talk show hosts and celebrities. You can use these methods too.

What are some of my own examples?

I burn all bridges equally when I'm backed into a corner. Once I was in a committee where all the group members despised me for unexplainable reasons. I tried everything I could to resolve the situation. When I failed and was more or less outcast, I tried something else. Like Griffin, I raised the ante and went for burning all bridges. And amazingly, this worked. When I unfairly criticized one person's policies, I made temporary allies from enemies of that person *in the moment*. I also started to get judged on things I did right rather than things I messed up. Though I did not make any long-time friends from all of this, I was backed into a corner and did what I could. Burning bridges helped me make effective change when I did have power.

The Leader's Dilemma

In relationships you wish to maintain—like a marriage or a job you like —you do not have the option to burn bridges. You may also face constraints in which strategies you can pursue due to legal repercussions (a boss has to be careful not to break workplace laws). In these situations, you may still be able to gain a strategic advantage by thinking about how the game is played.

Leaders often have to decide between great outcomes that might backfire and mediocre ones that work for sure. It is what I call "The Leader's Dilemma."

The issue stems in large part because the game has a fixed order. Because the leader has to act first, followers have time to observe flaws and make criticisms. Often, the good outcomes need cooperation so they are risky and less likely to win out. In turn, safer but mediocre outcomes rise to the top.

Why can't we all just get along?

Well, it turns out we sort of can. Here is an idea: if sequential play is the main cause of the problem, why not change that feature? Why not change the game into simultaneous play where players have to guess and commit to actions? Perhaps if all players moved without full knowledge, they can all be made better off on average. Indeed, this turns out to be a valuable option.

So let's get to the details. I want to illustrate the idea through a game I created about two retailers competing on clothing products. One business moves first and is the "leader." The other business is the "follower" and can threaten the good outcome with defection. What results in sequential play is a mediocre outcome for both businesses (there is another outcome with payoffs better for both parties—that is, the outcome is *Pareto dominated*).

The situation can be improved by changing the game into simultaneous play. In this case, each business has to guess at the other's actions, so they both will randomly commit to strategies. By shielding information, the leader business can produce a higher surplus for the group. On average, the surplus helps *all involved parties*. It is a classic win-win.

The Game—Sequential Play (Full Knowledge Of Action)

Imagine two businesses engaged in competition. The "leader" company moves first and announces whether it is creating a low-margin product (L) or a high-margin product (H). Upon observing the announcement, the "follower" business has two responses. It can either create an imitation product (I) under its own brand name, or it can just choose to match the product (M) by stocking it also.

You can think about the leader company as a brand name clothing retailer, and the follower company as a discount retailer, like Wal-Mart.

Assume the high-margin product has a market payoff of 4 million dollars, to be split between the two stores, and the low-margin product has one of 2 million dollars. Whenever the follower store chooses to match (M), the stores split the profits evenly.

The interesting part is when the follower store imitates (I). If the follower store imitates the high-margin product, the knock-off will actually be good enough to capture all orders and gain the entire market. On the other hand, if the follower store imitates the low-margin product, the knock-off will be so low quality that no one will buy it, allowing the leader store to capture the entire market. How does the game play out?

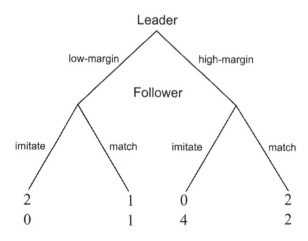

The Outcome

We can solve the game by using backwards induction. In this game, we need to imagine what the discount retailer will do in both low-margin and high-margin choices. Knowing what the discount retailer will choose will allow us to determine the best choice for the leader.

So let's analyze the game. What happens if the leader picks the low-margin scenario? In that case, we can read the tree to see the discount retailer will choose match (1) over imitate (0). Similarly, we can work through what happens in the high-margin scenario. In that case, the discount retailer will imitate (4) instead of match (2).

Now, knowing what the discount retailer will pick in each eventuality, the leader can choose accordingly. Picking the high-margin product leads to the discount retailer imitating and that gives a zero payoff (0) to the leader. On the other hand, picking the low-margin product leads to the discount retailer to match, providing a positive payoff (1) to the leader.

The logic indicates the leader will prefer to choose the low-margin product, to which the discount retailer imitates. The result is that both stores get a payoff of 1 million dollars. We can illustrate the solution on the game tree.

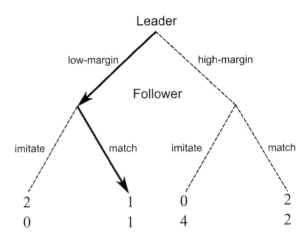

The Interpretation

The outcome is mediocre. Both stores end up with a payoff of 1 million dollars. If they instead could agree to split the high-margin product, they would both have 2 million dollars. This would be better for both sides.

While both sides would agree the outcome is better, there is a problem. There is no way to enforce getting to that outcome. If the leader picks the high-margin product, the follower would not match and split, but it would choose to imitate and capture the entire market.

The two companies might try to coordinate, but it could be hard to trust the other party and enforce the deal. If the game were repeated, say for hundreds of products, then both stores lose out over time.

How can they achieve a better outcome? One option is to change the sequential play into simultaneous play. The idea is to get the players to choose at the same time. This might be accomplished by hiring a mediator to collect strategy commitments. The second business needs to decide what it is doing *without knowing the first business's decision*.

The Revised Game—Simultaneous Play (No Knowledge Of Action)

The game will illustrate the benefit to limiting knowledge through simultaneous play. Because neither knows exactly how the other will respond, each will be forced to mix strategies. The result is higher average payouts—for both businesses. This is very useful if the game is repeated or played over several products. Simultaneous play can be represented by a matrix.

Follower

		Imitate	Match
Leader	Low-margin	2, 0	1, 1
	High-margin	0, 4	2, 2

The key feature is there is no pure strategy Nash equilibrium. If you try to figure out the best response, you will end up with a cycle.

For example, "low-margin" is best responded by "match," which is best responded by "high-margin," which is best responded by "imitate," which is best responded by "low-margin," and so on.

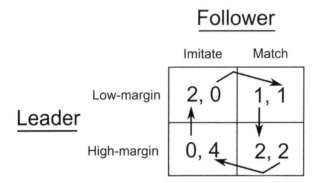

The situation is similar to the game of rock-paper-scissors. Every action is best responded by another action and players are never happy to stay put in one given outcome.

What's the answer? Just like in rock-paper-scissors, both players need to randomize strategies.

How do they do that? They will randomly choose actions until the opponent is indifferent between the pure strategy choices. An illustration: when you randomly mix the choice of rock, paper, and scissors in equal frequency, your opponent will win with equal chance by picking only rock, only paper, or only scissors.

In other games, the probability weights might not be equal. In this game, it turns out that player 1 will pick L with probability 2/3 (and H with probability 1/3) and player 2 will pick I with probability 1/3 (and M with probability 2/3).

I've included the equations at the end for completeness, as I will not go through the math here.

When all is said and done, both players will mix between their choices. What this does is it allows for some of the higher payoff outcomes to be included *for both players*. Sometimes players 1 or 2 capture the market entirely, and sometimes player 1 and 2 split the high and low outcomes. *They are not stuck in the one choice of splitting the low-margin market.*

As a consequence, the payoff to each player increases 33 percent from 1 million dollars to 1.33 million dollars, and both are better off.

Appendix: Mixed Equilibrium Math

Let's assume player 1 chooses *L* with probability *p* and *H* with probability $1 - p$. The probability will be set exactly so that player 2 is indifferent between the choices of *I* and *M*.

Payoff to I = Payoff to M

$$0p + 4(1 - p) = p + 2(1 - p)$$

$$4 - 4p = 2 - p$$

$$p = 2/3$$

Therefore, the payoff to playing *I* or *M* is $2 - p = 4/3$.

Now we solve for the mixed strategy of player 1. Assume player 2 chooses *I* with probability *q* and *M* with probability $1 - q$. The probability will be set exactly so that player 1 is indifferent between the choices of *L* and *H*.

Payoff to L = Payoff to H

$$2q + (1 - q) = 0q + 2(1 - q)$$

$$q + 1 = 2 - 2q$$

$$q = 1/3$$

Therefore, the payoff to playing *L* or *H* is $q + 1 = 4/3$.

Market Unraveling

This example is based on a paper from George Akerloff in 1966 about the market for bad used cars, cars colloquially called "lemons."

Imagine you're buying a used car using online car listings. You investigate the market and find listings ranging from $17,000 to $23,000. You are in email contact with the owners and you are trying to get the best deal. You are participating in a marketplace with smart buyers just like you. Which car are you likely to buy?

You think strategically. At first, you consider buying the cheapest listing to get a good deal. But soon you worry that a lower price might indicate lower quality. After all, sellers know more about their cars than you do. They must know the car is worth even less. That thought scares you, so you consider looking at the more expensive listings in the hope of getting better quality. But you soon realize that some sellers prey on this attitude. They intentionally list a bad car at a high price to scam you.

You cannot estimate the quality of any particular car, so you have to base your buying decision on the average quality of cars in the market. If cars are equally likely to be good or bad, then you might decide it is not worth paying more than the average price of cars that are listed. Initially cars are listed from $17,000 to $23,000, so you decide you will not pay more than the average of $20,000.

But this price limit has a negative consequence. A seller of a high-quality car would not want to sell a car for such a low value, and hence the seller would be driven out of the market.

In fact, all sellers who have cars valued over $20,000 would leave the market, as the following diagram illustrates.

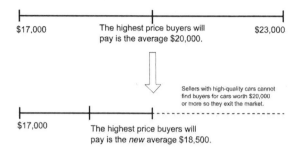

Once these sellers leave, the market is limited to car listings from $17,000 to $20,000. But at this stage, you face the same problem of quality. You still cannot estimate quality, so you again have a problem with how much to spend. You again decide you will not pay more than the average listing of $18,500 for a car. This move again drives sellers of high-quality cars out of the market.

The process continues over and over until the only sellers remaining have listings of $17,000. But there is a problem: the only cars that would sell for the minimum price would be the worst-quality and worst-maintained cars, most likely lemons. Most buyers do not want these cars, and so no one buys or sells anything. The market completely unravels, as illustrated in the following figure.

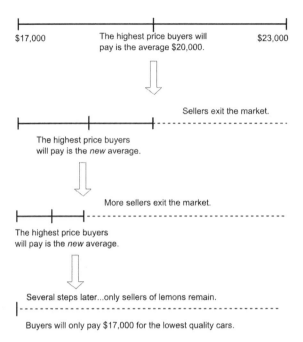

The highest price buyers will pay is the average $20,000.

$17,000

$23,000

Sellers exit the market.

The highest price buyers will pay is the *new* average.

More sellers exit the market.

The highest price buyers will pay is the *new* average.

Several steps later...only sellers of lemons remain.

Buyers will only pay $17,000 for the lowest quality cars.

Some Solutions

The model is fantastic, but it is not an accurate depiction. After all, used cars are still bought and sold—even high quality ones. The market for lemons is a theoretical concept, not necessarily a practical observation.

The used car market has developed protections to stop the market from unraveling. The main idea is to establish trust and improve a buyer's ability to recognize high-quality products. Tools such as car histories, warranties, and a national reputation (like CarMax) all improve a buyer's ability to judge quality. In game theory, an action or quality that can influence a belief is known as a *signal*.

We use signals all the time. A student that gets a college degree is not necessarily acquiring skills for a job. The student is signaling the ability to do analytic work for an employer. Similarly, people that buy designer clothes and expensive watches may hope to signal they are wealthy. By the same token, people can and do exploit the theory of signaling by falsifying academic records and buying clothes beyond their means. There is always a chance for the market to unravel; the market works because some signals are genuine and cannot be faked.

A Smart Pill

Imagine there is a magic pill that would improve your intelligence by 25 percent with no side effects. Would you take the pill?

Most people would probably jump on this idea. And in fact, there are definitely benefits to having a smarter society.

But I bet that most people would be taking the pill for the wrong reason. That is, they have not considered the strategic implications of the decision.

The Game Of Drugs

Consider the following scenario. You and I like to play chess for fun. We are currently equally skilled so that on average our games lead to draws or we trade off victories.

A pharmaceutical company releases a pill that improves intelligence, and trials have shown the pill improves chess performance.

Now each of us faces a choice to take the pill. If only one person takes the pill, that person is sure to win most of the games. If, however, both of us take it, then we both improve equally, and we are again at a competitive draw.

Here is what the game would look like.

	Your Choice	
My Choice	Pill	Don't
Pill	Draw	I Win
Don't	I Lose	Draw

How might this game play out?

Here is how I might think. I am a conservative person and would avoid taking a supplement pill if possible. And I know you are probably the same way. So it is possible that we could have a gentleman's agreement to avoid taking the pill.

But there is no way to enforce this. Each person is within his rights to take the pill and can do so secretly.

So suddenly, I begin to feel a doubt that you might take the pill. So I reason the following. If I alone take the pill, then I will be at a competitive advantage. If I take it and you do as well, then we will be equally matched which is fine.

Taking the pill is a safe strategic choice because it avoids the possibility that you alone take the pill and I get crushed in the game.

Ultimately both of us take the pill, even though neither of us wants to.

In Real Life

Does the above game sound too simplistic? In fact, the outcome mirrors the way that people actually think.

A pill that would make us smarter sounds like a good idea until the strategic implications are fully considered. A similar issue has plagued professional athletes who choose to take steroids or other drugs illegally.

It is important that we as a society stay cautious about performance enhancing drugs. Even those that do not want to take drugs are tempted to keep up with the competition.

A Voting Paradox

The idea that our choices are affected by other people's choices is a central component of game theory. It is also at the heart of any democracy: the laws you have to obey are a result of the preferences of everyone (well, everyone who voted anyway). This naturally leads into the topic of voting theory and the problem of trying to aggregate individual preferences into a group preference. To begin, a story from my childhood.

Growing up, I couldn't stand spicy food. My brother loved it. This was a constant source of conflict. If dinner was too spicy, I complained. If it was not spicy enough, my brother complained.

This is why my mom typically prepared separate portions of spicy and non-spicy food. But that was impractical for some dishes. Hence, one of us was often complaining that the other person was being favored. We tried to get "votes" from other family members to support our taste preference. It did not feel good to lose out.

Such situations are far from unusual. People are always complaining that they are the victim of an unfair majority, especially in situations when votes are collected. I think about situations like hiring decisions, the presidential election, and the baseball hall of fame. When you cannot get people to support your case, life can seem unfair and dictatorial.

But we should not be surprised. Situations where votes are collected are full of conflicting preferences. By their very nature, it is likely someone will feel shafted.

How often does this happen? Choice theory says it happens very frequently. There is a famous theorem about making optimal social decisions. It basically says that for many decisions (3 or more choices, 2 or more people), it is impossible to aggregate individual preferences in a meaningful way.

Here is how one graduate level-text summarizes the theorem: "Either we must give up the hope that societal preferences could be rational [in the economics sense] ... or we must accept dictatorship." (*Microeconomic Theory* by Andreu Mas-Colell, Michael D. Whinston, and Jerry R.

Green).

Before I get into a specific example, I'll digress about one of the great results from choice theory.

Arrow's Impossibility Theorem

Kenneth Arrow is an economist whose work I admire. He won the Nobel Memorial Prize in Economics at the age of 51, becoming the youngest ever recipient for the award. He made contributions to general equilibrium analysis, the economics of information, growth theory, and social choice theory.

I'm not the only one to admire his work. My friend's dad, an economist in Korea, admired Arrow so much that he was compelled to name his son Kenneth in honor. It is amusing because my friend Kenneth is sharp at economics and math, just like the economist he was named after. I'm not aware of any other people being named after economists.

I discuss Arrow in this article because he proved what he called a "general impossibility theorem." The theorem is so important that it is now named "Arrow's impossibility theorem" in his honor. This work is part of why he was awarded the National Medal in Science in 2004, the nation's most prestigious award for scientists. To give you a sense of Arrow's contributions, this theorem was just the beginning. I mean it literally was just the beginning of his research, as it was the topic of his Ph.D. Thesis.

The articulation and proof of the theorem are well beyond the scope of this book. The executive summary is that whenever there are at least 2 people and at least 3 options, it is impossible to aggregate individual preferences without violating some desired conditions. You either have to accept that society will not act rationally like an individual would, or you have to accept that society's preferences will exactly mimic one person's preferences. In a sense, that makes the individual a dictator.

You can get a sense of Arrow's theorem from a small-scale example, which I discuss next. The example also illustrates how voting problems were known almost two hundred years before Arrow. It is a philosophical idea that dates all the way back to the Enlightenment.

A Voting Paradox (Condorcet's Paradox)

In 1785, Marquis de Condorcet wrote one of his most important works, *Essay on the Application of Analysis to the Probability of Majority Decisions*. It was one of the first applications of probability to the social sciences, and it includes a stunning example of a possible problem with elections.

Imagine that there are three candidates running for office. I'll call them A, B, and C.

In this concocted example, let's just suppose there are only three voters (or there are three political constituencies, all voting in party line).

Each voter has a preference over the three candidates. I'll write the preferences in shorthand, with the most favored candidate first, and the least favored last.

Voter 1: A > B > C

Voter 2: B > C > A

Voter 3: C > A > B

For example, voter 1 prefers A the most, then B, and then C.

Which candidate best represents the majority preference?

Let's consider putting A in power. The result would be great news for voter 1, but both voters 2 and 3 would be unhappy as their candidates lost.

Voter 3 counters that the election is unfair. Voter 3 argues that C is a much better politician than A. This is clearly a biased opinion because voter 3 wants C to win it all. But voter 3 also discovers that voter 2 is unhappy. And that is the secret to the paradox.

Voters 2 and 3 meet and realize that they both prefer C over A. Take a look at the preferences to confirm.

Voter 1: A > B > C

Voter 2: B > **C > A**

Voter 3: **C > A** > B

Voter 3 has C as a first preference, and voter 2 has C as a second preference *over A*. This means both voters 2 and 3 would prefer C over A. So voters 2 and 3 decide that C would be a better person than A. They gang up and overrule voter 1, placing C in power.

The peace only lasts a few minutes because soon voter 2 has regrets about recommending C. Sure, C is better than A, but only by a little bit. In fact, voter 2 can only live with B being in power, his first preference. Is there a way to make that possible? Voter 2 decides to talk with voter 1, and soon learns something he likes. It turns out voter 1 also prefers B over C.

Voter 1: A > **B > C**

Voter 2: **B > C** > A

Voter 3: C > A > B

So voters 1 and 2 now combine forces to decide that B would be a better person than C. Using the power of majority, they gang up and place B in power. I'm sure you're getting the picture by now. B is in power for only a very short time when voters 1 and 3 join forces because they both prefer A over B.

Voter 1: **A > B** > C

Voter 2: B > C > A

Voter 3: C > **A > B**

And once again, the case is made to put A in power.

Using majority preference, it turns out that A loses to C, C loses to B, B loses to A, and A loses to C again, and so on *ad infinitum*. This is an example of how society's preferences are much more complicated than an individual's. Using the language of Arrow's Impossibility Theorem, the voting paradox would be an example of "irrational" societal preferences.

In this situation, no candidate can claim to be favored by the majority. It is impossible.

Now incorporate some real world practicalities: that people change their mind and are susceptible to miscalculations in snap decisions. That's the workings of a democracy. It is no wonder that people are always whining about something.

My Teacher's Clever Tissue Scheme

Even though individual preferences cannot *always* logically be translated into a satisfactory group decision, that should not stop you from trying. There are many incentives that can bring about tremendously positive outcomes for everyone.

My grade school teacher faced a problem that our classroom was generally short on facial tissues. The one school-supplied box was not nearly enough for 25 sniffling students. It was especially bad during allergy season and snowy days.

My third grade teacher devised an ingenious bribe. At the beginning of the year, he offered us 10 extra credit points if we brought in a box of facial tissue as part of our school supplies. Naturally all of us went home and begged our parents. And sure enough, nearly every single person showed up to class with a box of tissue paper, content to get 10 extra credit points.

Only years later did it dawn on me how clever this all was. Since all of us brought facial tissues, we were *all* getting 10 extra credit points. The net effect was that the extra credit had no beneficial impact on our grade.

The teacher's bribe was smart: the classroom was well-supplied with tissue paper, and none of the students at the time was wiser that the extra credit points had no value.

In fact, the real genius is that we had to bring in the tissue paper just to stay even with our classmates. Essentially my teacher capitalized on a game of escalation, which we will discuss in the next sections.

The Dollar Auction Game

Does today's pop music seem too loud and sound all the same? Do you have trouble hearing people in restaurant and bars? These phenomena are well known, but what is the motivation and cause for them? Below I give a game theory analogy that explains the behavior.

The "Who's Louder" Game

Two producers are competing to get his song played on the radio. The programmer will simply choose the song that sounds the loudest. What's the strategy for this game?

It is simple. Each producer will try to top the other person and mix his song a bit louder than the other. Not too loud as to be alarming, mind you. But just loud enough to catch the radio programmer's attention. Slowly but surely music will progressively get louder and louder. It sounds silly, but that is essentially what has happened to pop music in America.

NPR has an excellent and detailed article on the phenomenon, dubbed the loudness wars. The end result: pop music becomes louder and more homogenous. Scientists have confirmed this trend analytically by analyzing pop music over the last 50 years. Yes, it is now officially true that music is louder and all sounds the same.

The Dollar Auction Game

The music industry seems to have shot itself in the foot in a self-destructive war. The question is, if the end result was so predictable, why didn't the loudness wars stop earlier?

A useful analogy is the dollar auction game. Like many economics students, I learned about this game first-hand. My teacher described the game as a chance for us poor students to make a small profit, if we were smart enough.

The game involved my teacher auctioning off a dollar bill to the class. Bidding started at 5 cents and bids would increase by five cent increments. There were two main components to the auction.

1. The auction would end when no one bid higher. The highest bidder would pay the price of his bid and get the dollar as a prize.

2. The second highest bidder would also pay his bid (5 cents less than the winning bid) but get nothing in return.

My teacher justified the second rule as a reflection of true competition. In many contests, both sides end up paying or expending effort but only one gets the prize. He told us to think about lawsuits, sports competitions, and political donations. It made sense to us, and we soon started the game.

The bidding began at 5 cents and a hand shot up to claim the bid. Would anyone pay 10 cents? Another hand shot up. What about 15 cents? Again, another hand shot up. Bidding at this stage seemed harmless because it was an obvious deal to buy a dollar for any amount less.

The twist became clear about when the high bid was 75 cents. Many students started to think about how the second rule—the one requiring the loser to pay—would affect incentives. What might the second highest bidder think at this stage? He was offering 70 cents but being outbid. There were two choices he could make.

1. Do nothing and lose 70 cents if the auction ended.

2. Bid up to 80 cents, and if the auction ended, win the dollar, and profit 20 cents.

Between these two options, the better choice is to bid 80 cents with a chance to win rather than do nothing and lose for sure.

But this action has an effect on the person bidding 75 cents, who is now the second highest bidder. This person will now make a similar calculation. He can either stand pat and stand to lose 75 cents if the auction ends, or he can raise the bid to 85 cents and have a chance of profiting 15 cents. Again, bidding higher makes sense. Thinking more generally, it *always* makes sense for the second highest bidder to increase the bid.

Such strategy is why the game unraveled pretty quickly. Soon cash-strapped students were bidding *more* than one dollar and fighting over who would lose less money. It is the incentives that dictate this weird outcome. Consider an example when the highest bid is $1.50. Since the high bid is above the prize of $1, it is clear no new bidder will enter. Hence, the second bidder faces the two choices of doing nothing and losing at $1.45, or raising the bid to $1.55 to lose only 55 cents—if the auction ended and he recovered $1 from winning.

In this case, it makes just as much sense to limit loss as it does to seek profit. In any situation, the second highest bidder will raise the bid. This bidding war can theoretically continue indefinitely. In practical situations, it ends when someone folds.

In my class, the game ended around $2 when one player decided to end the madness. But talk to economics professors and you will hear that it is not unusual for the game to end at $5, $10, or even a larger amount. It is especially juicy if the two bidders dislike each other in social circles, and that adds its own element of entertainment. As a side note, the game can be played in other bid increments too, like 1 cent or 10 cents.

I think the game offers two insights. First, it is best to avoid such games from the outset. And second, if you find yourself in one, cut your losses early. It is better to lose at 2 cents than at 2 dollars.

The Loudness Game In Bars

The dollar auction game captures part of the strategy in the music loudness war: even though each person realized it was destructive to keep playing, each person felt justified in upping the ante to lose less.

Consider a related game. Two bars decide how loud to set their music. People will more often visit the louder bar. Again this is a simplistic way to view things. But it seems to model reality. In the game, each bar will jack up the volume ever so slightly to please customers, until the noise becomes deafeningly loud.

The *New York Times* covered the phenomenon of loud music inside restaurant and bars. Often noise level in bars was at dangerous levels over 85 decibels—louder than the sound from a subway train. Bars may even have a sinister reason for pushing the loudness. One study found that loud music can increase alcohol consumption.

Here is a table that illustrates the strategic similarities between the games.

	Pop Music	Dollar Auction	Music in Bars
Initial setting	Normal loudness	$0 bid	Normal loudness
Bidding war	Top other producers	Bid 1 cent more	Top other bars
Point of Danger	Loudness masks music quality	Bidding >$1 to avoid loss	Loudness above safe level 85 dB
End result	Homogenous music	Crazy bidding	Hearing loss
Who Profits?	Talentless musicians and producers	Auctioneer	Loud music could increase beer sales

None of these games works out well for the players. Here are some possible remedies in the dollar auction game and loudness wars.

1. Do Not Play The Game

The only way to avoid the trap of the dollar auction game is not to play. It is always tempting to join the game, but the ultimate bidding war is foreseeable, and one should stay away.

Similarly, one could try to avoid pop music and loud bars. But this is a bit harder in practice since we do not always have control over our environment.

2. Call For Regulation

If the government is justified in banning smoking to prevent second-hand smoke concerns, then perhaps it is justified in regulating the loudness of indoor places.

I say this with a big IF. I am not proposing this is an appropriate solution, as I think people should be entitled to listen to loud music, if they wish. I am only pointing out that regulation is a possible way to avoid the trap of indefinite escalation.

3. Get Earplugs

Your best response might be something you can control. Loud noises above 90 decibels can cause permanent hearing damage. I hope to preserve my senses as long as I can, and so I decide to play the game of music with a little bit of protection.

Sources

"The Loudness Wars: Why Music Sounds Worse." NPR. Web. 31 Dec. 2009. http://www.npr.org/2009/12/31/122114058/the-loudness-wars-why-music-sounds-worse

Buckley, Cara. "Working or Playing Indoors, New Yorkers Face an Unabated Roar." *New York Times.* Web. 19 Jul. 2012. http://www.nytimes.com/2012/07/20/nyregion/in-new-york-city-indoor-noise-goes-unabated.html

Dean, Jeremy. "Why Loud Music in Bars Increases Alcohol Consumption." PsyBlog. 17 Sept. 2008. Web. http://www.spring.org.uk/2008/09/why-loud-music-in-bars-increases.php

Waiting In Line, High Heels, And Studying For Finals

Now, here, you see, it takes all the running you can do, to keep in the same place—Alice in Wonderland

At first glance, queuing, fashion, and education are very different topics. And yet, surprisingly they are similar from a game theory perspective. In short, these are all arguably examples of failed cooperation due to the individual incentive to escalate.

I will explain what I mean by this in detail below. For now, let's consider the game of waiting in line.

Why Do We Wait In Line?

On the opening night of a blockbuster movie, I went to the theater to see the show. To make sure we got good seats, we showed up an hour early.

But guess what? We weren't even the first people in line! At least 10 people decided it was better to stand in line even earlier.

While I waiting in the line, I thought about how wasteful it was to wait for the movie. Here we were just standing around on a perfectly good Friday night when we could have been doing something fun instead.

Why does this happen? This is not hard to understand from a game theory perspective.

The game of waiting in line is defined by two strategic considerations. One aspect is that waiting in line is boring, and waiting for a longer time is a waste of time. The other aspect is that people who show up early can pick better seats, so clearly one would want to show up before the crowds.

If everyone simply showed up at the movie near its show time, then there would be no line and seats would be chosen nearly randomly. So everyone gets the payoff of sitting in an average seat.

But this cannot be an equilibrium. Someone will decide to defect from the group and show up 5 minutes early. I mean why not? Rather than showing up on time and getting an *average* seat, you could show up early and get the *best* seat in the house. That's certainly worth 5 minutes of waiting.

Of course, this logic will appeal to many moviegoers, and so it ends up being the case that lots of people show up 5 minutes early. Suddenly the game has changed: now so many people show up 5 minutes early, that showing up 5 minutes early only gets you an average seat!

And so, repeating the logic one would consider showing up 10 minutes early, then 15 minutes early, and so on. It is not totally uncommon to have people camp out hours or even a whole day for the opening of a huge blockbuster.

The result is an extremely wasteful equilibrium. People will wait in lines for a movie merely because *everyone else is waiting in line too*.

What we have here is a failure of coordination.

In theory, theaters could eliminate movie theater lines altogether. Theaters could simply assign seats or make it illegal for people to show up early. Or, they could equally as well assign seats at random: as people showed up, their ticket could be scanned and they would be assigned a seat.

But unlike Southwest Airlines—that makes money on priority seating with EarlyBird Check-in—theaters make money by not selling priority seats. Theaters are happy to encourage long lines, which generate buzz and likely increase concession sales for hungry and bored moviegoers waiting in line.

So the game of waiting in line is driven by consumer escalation that profits the theaters. As I'll explain next, this is the same type of game for why people might wear high heels.

High Heels: Who Is Tallest?

Can you see the connection between waiting in line and wearing high heels?

Women could all agree not to wear high heels. Each person would walk proudly in comfortable shoes and stand at her natural height, and not bear the expense of buying a shoe.

But if everyone did this, there is a natural temptation for someone to defect from the group. One woman is going to think it is advantageous to wear shoes with a little lift to look taller and be more attractive.

When a few women start wearing high heels, it becomes more tempting that other women would want to wear them as well.

Eventually everyone feels it is sensible to wear high heels. Notice the connection with waiting in line: people are doing something wasteful only because everyone else is doing it too.

Fashion designers could agree not to make high heeled shoes, knowing that they are uncomfortable and make it hard for women to walk. There is even some evidence that high heeled shoes are genuinely unhealthy and can cause long term damage to toes, tendons, and bones.

But designers, like movie theaters, are fine with the current situation and lack of consumer coordination.

Students Could Cooperate, But They Do Not

I loved the time I was a student at Stanford, particularly in the great weather of Spring Quarter.

The only problem, as they say, was that classes got in the way. On a given afternoon, I was far more likely to be studying under the fluorescent light at the library than basking in the sun at the lovely outdoor swimming pool.

A couple times I did question my choice. Why was I studying the arcane subject of analysis on manifolds instead of going outside? I mean, I'd likely forget the material in a couple of years, so I might as well skip studying and enjoy the weather.

There was definitely a great opportunity for collusion. My math class only had about 8 students. If we all met one day, we could have agreed to study very little for exams. The result would be that we'd all end up getting about the same score (being nearly equally smart). And since the class was graded on a generous curve, we'd all end up with about a B+ for doing very little work!

By now you can deduce why this plan would be hard to execute. There is always some type A personality that would agree to the plan but then secretly study and ruin the curve. Knowing that one person wanted to study meant it was necessary for the rest of us to study as well to avoid getting a bad grade.

Just like in the examples of waiting in line and wearing high heels, there was a circularity to our logic. Again, we were all studying for this final because we knew that everyone else was studying too.

This is a game that is a "wasteful" equilibrium for the students, but one with positive results for society. Professors are happy to impart their knowledge (without classes they'd be out of a job!), and society benefits as more individuals get educated.

Summary

Here is a table that shows how the phenomena are similar.

	Waiting in line	Wearing high heels	Studying for finals
Cooperate	Show up showtime Get average seat	Wear normal shoes Stand natural height	Avoid studying Get curved grade
Reason to Defect	Show up early Get best seat	Wear shoes with lift Be taller, sexier	Study more Get better grade
Escalation	Show up earlier	Fit in with fashion	Studying more
Wasteful Result	Lines are boring	Heels hurt Bad for health	Studying is boring
Who benefits?	Theaters sell food	Designers sell shoes	Professors teach Society educated

How To Win

Each of these games shows an example of failed coordination, resulting in a wasteful outcome for people playing the game.

The horrible part is this: the best strategy in these games is to be more ruthless, more destructive, and more wasteful than other players. For example, it is the person who camps out the longest who gets the best seat, the woman who wears the fanciest/most expensive high heels who often has the best fashion, and the student that studies day and night who often gets the best grade.

It was a long time ago I figured out how to beat these people. You should not try to beat them at their own game. If you're not winning the game you are playing, you must change the game and play by your own rules.

A few strategies for these games are:

--Wait for a movie to get less popular and lines die down.

--Forget movie theaters altogether, just wait for home video.

--Ignore fashion and avoid high heels.

--Study a specified amount of time, then have fun.

--Learn for its own sake, not for the grade.

None of these strategies is mind-blowing or would appeal to the masses. But they allow you to spend time productively while others waste time in lines, hurt their bodies, and lose their memorized facts. Perhaps you can win if you play your own game.

I play for the long run, and I will find a way to win this game.

Jealousy

Most of the examples in this book assume that each person is hoping to get the best possible individual outcome and does not really care what other people get. That means that if everyone can get richer in absolute terms, that is better than everyone being poorer, or one person being mildly wealthy. However, this is clearly not true as jealousy is a part of life. This example is about how jealousy affects how people play games.

Let's you and I play this very simple game. Imagine we are playing this game in a college experiment. We each have a chance to win money depending on how we play, with the following rules.

--You and I each secretly play "A" or "B."

--If we both pick "A," then we each get $4.

--If one person picks "A," and the other "B", the person picking "A" gets $1 and the person playing "B" gets $3.

--If we both pick "B," then we each get no money and leave with $0.

Here is the matrix of payouts.

		Your Choice	
		A	B
My Choice	A	4, 4	1, 3
	B	3, 1	0, 0

Which option would you pick if the game is played only once?

Analyzing The Game

This game is a no-brainer: it is a *dominant* strategy to pick "A" and both of us should get $4.

Verifying this is an easy task. Each person thinks about the best response to the other player's move. If the other player picks "A," then it is best to also pick "A" to get $4 rather than "B" to get $3. If the other player picks "B," it is also better to pick "A" and get $1 rather than "B" to get $0.

The best strategy is to pick "A," regardless of what the other person is doing. Both players should easily cooperate and get $4.

There is no sensible reason to pick "B." And yet, that is exactly what researchers found people doing over half a century ago, in a similar game played with pennies rather than dollars. The results were astounding: **more than 50 percent ended up playing the strategy "B"**!

It could have been possible people did not understand the rules, or they did not take it seriously when playing for pennies. But the researchers raised another possibility from a biological perspective.

The Green-Eyed Monster Of Jealousy

As explained above, both players maximize their payout when they pick "A." It should be obvious that picking "A" is the best thing to do. Except, perhaps we are thinking about the problem with the wrong motivation.

In game theory, economics, or business, we often choose the option that brings us the highest profit in absolute terms. All things equal, we would rather have $1,000 than $100.

But people do not always think in absolute success. They can sometimes think in terms of relative success: the goal is not to maximize payout, but rather, in the researchers' words, "to maximize the difference between one's self and the other player."

There is further experimental evidence of this idea, as explained on Michael Shermer's blog. Consider a hypothetical situation where you could earn $50,000 when other people earned $25,000. Would you prefer that, or would you prefer a situation where you earned $100,000 and others earned $250,000? You might think it is better to earn $100,000 since that means you can enjoy twice as many goods. However, Shermer points out most people would prefer the first option of making less in absolute terms but having a higher relative ranking in society.

The point is that relative thinking, and jealousy of other people's success, factors into how people think about money.

The Destructive Nature Of Relative Thinking

The original payout matrix reflected total payouts. But imagine that people were thinking in terms of *relative* rather than *absolute* payouts. The game is now transformed into the following rules.

>--If we both pick "A," then we each get $0 more than the other person.

>--If one person picks "A," and the other "B", the person picking "B" gets $2 more than the other player.

>--If we both pick "B," then we each get no money and also leave with $0 more than the other person.

Here is the matrix of relative payouts.

Your Choice

		A	B
		A	B
My Choice	A	0, 0	-2, 2
	B	2, -2	0, 0

The payouts of this game are completely changed from the original one. Notice how the original game—which was non-zero sum and mutually profitable—is now suddenly a zero sum, and competitive, game.

The strategy becomes competitive too: in this game, it is a dominant strategy to pick "B," meaning both players are expected to leave with nothing.

Rather than cooperating for mutual gain, both players "happily" end up with nothing to avoid letting the other person gain in stride.

Get Over Your Money Jealousy

This outcome is sadly not just theoretical: people gleefully act towards mutual destruction out of money jealousy.

I have my own personal analogy to get over jealousy. I think about success as filling up water flowing from an ocean. Each of us has a different size glass that represents a personal level of achievement. There is really no point worrying if your neighbor has a bigger glass than you since there is more than enough water to go around. If you want to get more, then focus on what you can do. Success will come from building your own glass and filling it, not from shattering what your neighbor has. It is time to put the green eyed monster of jealousy to rest.

Mind Your Decisions

Sources

"Some Descriptive Aspects of Two-Person Non-Zero-Sum Games. II." J. Sayer Minas, Alvin Scodel, David Marlowe and Harve Rawson *The Journal of Conflict Resolution* Vol. 4, No. 2 (Jun., 1960), pp. 193-197. Available at http://www.jstor.org/stable/172653

Why People Believe Weird Things About Money. Michael Shermer. Jan 2008. Web. http://www.michaelshermer.com/2008/01/weird-things-about-money/

Credit: I came across this game in the book *The Survival Game.*

Conclusion

Game theory is the study of strategic situations. In the classroom, game theory means understanding mathematical games, developing models of games, and solving for Nash equilibria. The games studied in the classroom will never capture the complexity of situations in life. Nevertheless, I hope this book has demonstrated how we often face situations similar to models in game theory, and we can use the insights from the game to have an appreciation for why people act in certain ways and why many bad outcomes are the result of coordination failures.

But we do not need to stop there. If you do not like the outcome of the game, then it is time to start playing a new game. The second section of this book was all about understanding strategies to change the game to create cooperation and better outcomes for everyone. Game theory helps us appreciate that we cannot dictatorially impose changes on society, as the micro-motives of everyone responding to the rule changes can lead to unexpected macro-behavior. We must always be on the lookout for the role of jealousy and games of escalation that tempt people to expend effort destructively or wastefully. I mean how much time have you wasted in your life waiting in line?

I hope that understanding game theory can help you understand and then tackle the strategic situations you will face in your life.

Of course, this book is just an introduction. Here are a few of the books I recommend for further study.

Thinking Strategically by Avinash Dixit and Barry Nalebuff. This is my favorite book about game theory and it is accessible to the lay reader. Also read the follow-up **The Art of Strategy**, the updated 2008 version.

Co-Opetition by Adam Brandenburger and Barry Nalebuff. This is a business book explaining many applications of game theory. It introduced me to the concept of "changing the game."

Game Theory: An Introduction by Steve Tadelis. This is a textbook on game theory suitable for an advanced undergraduate. I learned game theory from Professor Tadelis and highly recommend this book.

Game Theory 101 by William Spaniel. This is a best-selling and accessible introduction to game theory based on William Spaniel's popular YouTube series *Game Theory 101*.

Gaming the Vote by William Poundstone. The book is about the game theory of voting, full of interesting historical examples.

Game Theory at Work by James Miller. This is a book with many examples of real-life strategic situations.

A Beautiful Mind by Sylvia Nasar. This is a biography of John Nash, the "father" of non-cooperative game theory.

Game Theory Evolving by Herbert Gintis. This is an excellent introduction to game theory that also includes a discussion of evolutionary applications.

The Compleat Strategyst by John D. Williams. This is a 1954 book on zero-sum games published by the RAND Institute.

Game Theory by Drew Fudenberg and Jean Tirole. This is a graduate level text on game theory for serious study of the subject.

The Strategy of Conflict by Thomas Schelling. This book was first published in 1960 and discusses game theory in a political context of deterrence. It introduced the idea of focal points.

Insights into Game Theory: An Alternative Mathematical Experience by Ein-Ya Gura and Michael Maschler. This book has clear explanations of the stable matching problem, Arrow's Impossibility Theorem, the Shapley value, and the Talmud bankruptcy problem.

Playing for Real: A Text on Game Theory by Ken Binmore. This textbook is a great and comprehensive introduction to game theory.

Luck, Logic, and White Lies: The Mathematics of Games by Jorg Bewersdorff. This book explains the mathematics of games of chance, combinatorial games, and games of strategy.

Games of Strategy: Theory and Applications by Melvin Dresher. This is a 1961 book on zero-sum games. It is highly technical but will be interesting to someone that enjoys linear algebra.

Putting Auction Theory to Work by Paul Milgrom. This is a textbook on auction theory suitable for an advanced undergraduate course.

Theory of Games and Economic Behavior by John von Neumann and Oskar Morgenstern. This is the classic 1944 text that developed utility and game theory rigorously from axioms and set theory.

More from Presh Talwalkar

Math Puzzles Volume 1: Classic Riddles And Brain Teasers In Counting, Geometry, Probability, And Game Theory. This book contains 70 interesting brain-teasers.

Math Puzzles Volume 2: More Riddles And Brain Teasers In Counting, Geometry, Probability, And Game Theory.

Math Puzzles Volume 3: Even More Riddles And Brain Teasers In Geometry, Logic, Number Theory, And Probability.

But I only got the soup! This fun book discusses the mathematics of splitting the bill fairly.

40 Paradoxes in Logic, Probability, and Game Theory. Is it ever logically correct to ask "May I disturb you?" How can a football team be ranked 6th or worse in several polls, but end up as 5th overall when the polls are averaged? These are a few of the thought-provoking paradoxes covered in the book.

Multiply By Lines. It is possible to multiply large numbers simply by drawing lines and counting intersections. Some people call it "how the Japanese multiply" or "Chinese stick multiplication." This book is a reference guide for how to do the method and why it works.

The Best Mental Math Tricks. Can you multiply 97 by 96 in your head? Or can you figure out the day of the week when you are given a date? This book is a collection of methods that will help you solve math problems in your head and make you look like a genius.

About The Author

Presh Talwalkar studied Economics and Mathematics at Stanford University. His site *Mind Your Decisions* has blog posts and original videos about math that have been viewed millions of times.